AIR WAR OVER NORTH VIETNAM

OPERATION ROLLING THUNDER, 1965–1968

STEPHEN EMERSON

Pen & Sword
MILITARY

First published in Great Britain in 2018 by
PEN AND SWORD MILITARY
an imprint of
Pen and Sword Books Ltd
47 Church Street
Barnsley
South Yorkshire S70 2AS

Maps by George Anderson
Typeset by Aura Technology and Software Services, India
Printed and bound by CPI Group (UK) Ltd, Croydon, CR0 4YY

ISBN 978 1 52670 822 9

Pen & Sword Books Ltd incorporates the imprints of Pen & Sword
Archaeology, Atlas, Aviation, Battleground, Discovery, Family History, History, Maritime, Military,
Naval, Politics, Railways, Select, Social History, Transport, True Crime, Claymore Press, Frontline
Books, Leo Cooper, Praetorian Press, Remember When, Seaforth Publishing and Wharncliffe.

For a complete list of Pen and Sword titles please contact
Pen and Sword Books Limited
47 Church Street, Barnsley, South Yorkshire, S70 2AS, England
email: enquiries@pen-and-sword.co.uk
website: www.pen-and-sword.co.uk

CONTENTS

List of Maps

GLOSSARY

AGM-12	Bullpup air-to-ground missile with 250-pound warhead
AGM-45	Shrike air-to-ground homing missile with 150-pound warhead
AGM-62	Walleye air-to-ground guided missile with 825-pound warhead
AIM-7	Sparrow air-to-air missile
AIM-9	Sidewinder air-to-air missile
alpha strike	large-scale air strike against a fixed target
Annam	The central region of the Vietnamese peninsula centered on Hue.
armed recce	roaming air patrol seeking out targets of opportunity
Atoll missile	air-to-air missile used by MiG-21s that was a Soviet copy of the U.S. AIM-9 Sidewinder missile
CAG	Carrier Air Group commander; senior officer in charge of all squadrons aboard an aircraft carrier. Term was retained even after Navy changed from Carrier Air Groups to Carrier Air Wings.
Cochin China	The far southern region of the Vietnamese peninsula with Saigon at its center.
CVW	Carrier Air Wing; composed of all squadrons assigned to an aircraft carrier. Every aircraft carrier had its own unique numbered air wing, e.g., CVW-2, under command of a CAG.
Dixie Station	Code name for Navy carrier operating point in the South China Sea that supported ground operations in South Vietnam.
DMZ	demilitarized zone dividing North and South Vietnam
ECM	electronic countermeasures
Iron Hand	SAM suppression mission
MAAG	Military Assistance Advisory Group; absorbed by MACV in 1964
MACV	Military Assistance Command Vietnam; established 1962
MK-81	250-pound bomb
MK-82	500-pound bomb
MK-82 Snakeye	500-pound bomb equipped with stabilizing fins for low-level bombing
MK-83	1,000-pound bomb
MK-84	2,000-pound bomb
M118	Air Force 3,000-pound bomb
NFL	National Liberation Front; short form of the National Front for the Liberation of the South
NSC	National Security Council (U.S.)
Operation Barrel Roll	Northern Laos operating area; part of U.S. interdiction effort
Operation Bolo	January 1967 Air Force operation to lure out North Vietnamese MiG fighters

Operation Neutralize	U.S. air, naval, and artillery bombardment of North Vietnamese artillery positions just north of the DMZ from September to October 1967.
Operation Niagara	U.S. defense of the Marine base at Khe Sanh from January to April 1968.
Operation Steel Tiger	Southern Laos operating area; part of U.S. interdiction effort
Operation Tiger Hound	Southern Laos operating area along South Vietnamese northwest border that fell under MACV control.
PLAF	People's Liberation Armed Forces, better known as the Viet Cong
POL	petroleum, oil, and lubricants
prohibited zone	A 10 nautical mile (11.5 mile) circular zone around Hanoi and a 4 nautical mile (4.6 mile) circular zone around Haiphong that were off limits to bombing without special presidential approval.
restricted zone	A 30 nautical mile (34.5 mile) circular zone around Hanoi and a 10 nautical mile (11.5 mile) circular zone around Haiphong that were off limits to bombing without special Joint Chiefs approval.
Route Package	Also called Route Pack. A geographic operating area of North Vietnam; numbered I to V plus VI A and VI B.
SA-2	Soviet-made Guideline surface-to-air missile
SAM	surface-to-air missile
Shrike	air-to-ground homing missile with 400-pound warhead; officially AGM-45
TF-77	Task Force 77; naval carrier task force component of Seventh Fleet
TFS	tactical fighter squadron (Air Force)
TFW	tactical fighter wing (Air Force)
Tonkin	The far northern region of the Vietnamese peninsula with Hanoi at its center.
TRS	tactical reconnaissance squadron (Air Force)
VA	attack squadron (Navy)
VF	fighter squadron (Navy)
VNAF	Republic of Vietnam Air Force (South Vietnam)
VPAF	Vietnamese People's Air Force (North Vietnam)
Walleye	air-to-ground guided missile with 825-pound warhead; officially AGM-62
Wild Weasel	F-100F and F-105F SAM suppression aircraft (Air Force)
Yankee Station	Code name for Navy carrier operating point in the Gulf of Tonkin that supported air operations in North Vietnam, Laos, and occasionally in South Vietnam.
Zuni rockets	5-inch air-to-ground rockets used by Navy and VNAF aircraft

North and South Vietnam, 1964.

1. A PLACE CALLED VIETNAM

Few places in Asia, other than possibly the Korea peninsula, have been as severely buffeted by the unpredictable winds of the Cold War than Vietnam. As with Korea, Vietnam would pull the United States into a conflict it never wanted, understood or was prepared to fight. Despite an overwhelming commitment of American lives and treasure, victory on the battlefield in Vietnam would also be just as elusive for the United States. More significantly, the Vietnam experience would have a profound impact on the American national psyche and U.S. foreign and military policy that still endures today.

It wasn't always this case, for in the summer of 1964 most Americans were more preoccupied with a presidential campaign and the recently passed civil rights legislation than in developing events in far off Southeast Asia in a place called Vietnam. This was somewhat surprising given the critical post-World War II role of the United States in supporting French military efforts to quash Ho Chi Minh's communist nationalist insurgency. It is even more telling as Americans came perilously close to being drawn directly into war ten years earlier as the besieged French garrison at Dien Bien Phu battled for its life. Ultimately, American combat troops would indeed be committed to a war in Southeast Asia when 3,500 men of the 9th Marine Expeditionary Brigade waded ashore at Da Nang, South Vietnam on March 8, 1965.

The Legacy of French Indochina

The roots of America's military intervention in Vietnam can be traced back some 20 years previous to the end of World War II as France sought to reestablish control over its former colonial empire in Indochina in the face of rising Vietnamese nationalism. Critically, this re-conquest, for that is surely what it was, would set in motion a series of events that would steadily pull the United States deeper into war through a series of escalating commitments and by placing American prestige and leadership in Southeast Asia on the line. Just as unexpectedly too, the conflict in Vietnam would grow to become a central flashpoint in the Cold War for the next three decades.

The French involvement in Southeast Asia can be traced back to the height of European imperialism and colonial expansion at the end of the 19th century. From an established presence in Saigon and Cochin China at the southern end of the Vietnamese peninsula, the French rapidly expanded their presence northward in the 1880s and 1890s to include the Annam (central) and Tonkin (northern) regions of Vietnam, as well as all of present-day Cambodia and Laos to form the Indochinese Union, more commonly known as French Indochina. With this vast territory under French rule, French administrators sought to exploit the wealth and labor of Indochina for the greater good of France while maintaining a degree of peace and stability by coopting local elites and suppressing dissent. The Japanese military occupation of Indochina in September 1940 brought not only an end to this state of affairs, but also energized a growing sense of indigenous nationalism and self-determination that was stoked by the Allies in their all-out effort to defeat Japan.

American Office of Special Services (predecessor to the CIA) officers supported Ho Chi Minh and his nationalist Viet Minh forces against the Japanese occupation of Vietnam during World War II.

Thus, not surprisingly, Ho Chi Minh and his Indochinese Communist Party unilaterally declared the creation of the Democratic Republic of Vietnam in Hanoi, as the Japanese were signing their formal surrender on September 2, 1945 aboard the USS *Missouri* in Tokyo Bay. Naturally this did not go over well with the French who were planning their post-war return. With the help of British forces, France systematically reoccupied Cochin China and reestablished control over most southern cities by the end of 1945. Following negotiations with the Chinese Nationalists, who secured the area north of the 16th parallel under terms of the Potsdam Conference, French forces also began returning to Tonkin in the north in March 1946. The situation was tense however, as an uneasy modus vivendi prevailed. Viet Minh forces would remained ensconced in parts of Hanoi and Haiphong alongside French troops as negotiations proceeded over the future of Vietnamese independence.

This put the United States in quite a quandary. Should it throw its weight behind Ho Chi Minh, who fought with Allied forces against the Japanese occupation in the name of Vietnamese self-determination and the late President Franklin Roosevelt's anti-colonialist principles? Or should it support the imperial aspirations in Southeast Asia of France, a vital yet fragile ally that would be critical in stemming the spread of communism in post-war Europe? Initially the Truman administration sought to walk a fine line between the two positions by labelling Indochina an internal French matter, while tactfully trying to nudge Paris to grant more self-government and increased autonomy to the people of the region. In the end, however, the strategic importance of strengthening the Franco–American relationship and resisting the global tide of communism expansion forced Truman's hand.

N

CHINA

CHINA

TONKIN
1885

1888

● Hanoi

1888

LAOS

Gulf

of

Tonkin

CHINA

Vientiane ●

French sphere
of influence

ANNAM

1893

1874

Hue ●

SIAM-THAILAND

LAOS

● Bangkok

LAOS
1893

LAOS
1893

CAMBODIA
1904

ANNAM
1904

CAMBODIA

1863

ANNAM

Gulf

Phnom Penh ●

of

1862

Thailand

● Saigon

1867

COCHIN
CHINA

0   50   100   150   200 kms

The making of French Indochina.

The French defeat at Dien Bien Phu and the signing of the Geneva Peace Accords in 1954 signaled the ending of France's involvement in Vietnam, but created a political and military void that the United States reluctantly began to fill.

Moreover, with the outbreak of fighting between the Viet Minh and French in Hanoi in December 1946 the die was cast. The First Indochina war had begun and the Americans would throw their full support behind France. What was once a campaign of French colonial reconquest would quickly become an internationalized Cold War battleground, sucking the United States, China, and the Soviet Union into its deadly vortex. Ultimately, the capitulation of the French garrison at Dien Bien Phu in May 1954 and the signing of the Geneva Peace Accords in July 1954 would be the closing act for French Indochina. Peace would remain elusive however, as would the fate of Vietnamese people with the former colony expediently partitioned in two at the 17th parallel to create two competing poles of power. Ho Chi Minh's Democratic Republic of Vietnam controlled the territory to the north, while the French-created State of Vietnam controlled the territory to the south. More important, the French withdrawal would set the stage for American entry into an even wider and more deadly conflict in the next decade.

Passing the Torch

Following the collapse of French Indochina, the United States had become the de facto guarantor of South Vietnamese independence and in Washington's view the lynchpin against the rising tide of unchecked communist aggression in Southeast Asia. Not only was the State of Vietnam and the now independent states of Laos and Cambodia directly threatened, but neighboring Thailand was vulnerable and possibly even Indonesia and the Philippines were under threat. If the south of Vietnam fell to the communists the remaining countries of the region were likely to fall like dominos. As U.S. Secretary of State John Foster Dulles declared in July 1954, "The thing from now on is not to mourn the past but to seize the future opportunity to prevent the loss of northern Vietnam from leading to the expansion of Communism throughout Southeast Asia and the Southwest Pacific."[1] Everything possible now needed to be done by the Eisenhower administration to prevent this from happening.

American aid had already been flowing into Indochina since 1950 in support of the French war effort and by the time of Dien Bien Phu the United States had supplied some $1.5 billion in economic and military assistance.[2] Enormous quantities of war matériel—including uniforms, small arms, munitions, and more than 30,000 trucks, 1,800 combat vehicles, nearly 500 aircraft, and even two World War II-vintage aircraft carriers—had failed to stem the tide of the communist Viet Minh advance. But now things were going to be different as Washington moved to fortify the Saigon regime as a bulwark against the communist onslaught. The first direct U.S. military aid began to arrive in Saigon in January 1955 along with an expanded training and advisory role for the U.S. Military Assistance Advisory Group (MAAG). The Americans were now taking charge.

In Ngo Dinh Diem the Americans found their man following his overthrow of the French-installed chief of state, the former emperor Bao Dai, in October 1955 and the creation of the Republic of Vietnam, more commonly known as South Vietnam. Although an ardent Francophile, Diem was glad to see the discredited French depart the scene and seize this new opportunity for advancing Vietnamese independence. He was also a strident anti-communist and authoritarian leader who rarely hesitated to crush his political opponents, both communist and non-communist alike. By the late 1950s Diem had stamped out the most visible opposition to his rule and driven the remaining elements underground, all the while touting the "democratic miracle" that was unfolding in South Vietnam. Although not always approving of Diem's and his inner family circle's strong-arm tactics, Washington nonetheless welcomed the sense of stability he brought to the country and his no-nonsense, hardline stance against the communist north.

Despite some reservations about the growing level of American involvement in Vietnam within parts of the U.S. government during the late 1950s and early 1960s, the Cold War was in full swing and Washington was bent on drawing an increasingly hard line in the

The powerful Secretary General of the Vietnamese Communist party and a close confidant of Ho Chi Minh, Le Duan, pushed an aggressive war policy in the south even at the risk of bringing the Americans directly into the conflict.

Vice-President Lyndon Johnson and his wife visit Saigon in May 1961 to push political and social reforms to counter the growing Viet Cong insurgency, but the increasingly dictatorial South Vietnamese President, Ngo Dinh Diem (front right) and his sister-in-law, Madam Nhu (front center), would have none of it. (Photo LBJ Library)

sand—at the 17th parallel in the case of Vietnam. The tap began to flow in 1955 with an initial American aid package totaling $320 million and between 1955 and 1960 the United States would provide almost $2 billion in military and economic assistance to South Vietnam.[3] The bulk of this assistance, some $1.5 billion, was directed toward building a military capable of thwarting any attempted northern invasion of the south. Thanks to American money, equipment, and training the outgoing MAAG commander was proud to claim in August 1960 that the North Vietnamese in 1954 could have "walked into Saigon standing up [but] today if they tried it, they would have one nasty fight on their hands."[4]

The escalating American commitment to the Saigon government, however, was met in kind with a rising commitment to the Hanoi government from China and the Soviet Union. Ho Chi Minh signed a friendship treaty with the Chinese in June 1955 and soon afterward Chinese technicians were heavily involved in post-war reconstruction projects. Between 1955 and 1960 some $225 million in Chinese aid flowed into North Vietnam. Likewise, Hanoi was able to obtain $100 million in economic aid from Moscow, as well as its assistance with the North's industrialization efforts.[5]

Even as Ho Chi Minh was focused on securing the communist revolution in the north, many relocated Viet Minh from the south were clamoring for more aggressive action against the Diem government. Secretary General Le Duan, a former southern Viet Minh leader himself, had been pushing party leaders to be more supportive of the revolution in the south. He was finally successful in September 1960 with the party's Central

Chronology: August 1945– March 1965

1945

August 14	Japan unconditionally surrenders ending World War II in the Pacific.
September 2	Ho Chi Minh proclaims Vietnamese independence establishing the Democratic Republic of Vietnam.

1946

November	French forces oust Viet Minh from Haiphong and Hanoi in heavy fighting.
December	First Indochina war begins. France commits 50,000 men.
1947–1948	Sporadic fighting; French Union Forces control all major cities. Viet Minh withdraw to countryside.
	In late 1947 Battle of Bac Cam. Viet Minh defeated, but majority of their forces escape into the jungle.

1949

March	State of Vietnam is established by the French with former Emperor Bao Dai as chief of state with capital in Saigon.
	Vietnamese National Army for the State of Vietnam created later the same year.
1952	Bitter fighting in the north, especially along border with China. Viet Minh regroups westward toward Laos to re-establish supply lines.

1954

March 30 to May 7	Battle of Dien Bien Phu. French garrison is forced to capitulate; some 10,000 French Union Forces are captured.
July	Geneva Conference begins to decide future of Indochina. Partition of Vietnam along the 17th parallel with national elections to be held by July 1956.
October	French depart Hanoi and Ho Chi Minh triumphantly enters the city.
	Nearly 1 million Catholics flee the north for the south.
	Ngo Dinh Diem appointed prime minister of the State of Vietnam by Bao Dai.

1955

January	First direct U.S. military aid to Bao Dai government arrives.
October	Ngo Dinh Diem launches coup and takes power. Proclaims the Republic of Vietnam (South Vietnam).

1956

April	French high command in Saigon is disestablished and last French troops depart South Vietnam.

1959

July 8	First attack on U.S. military advisers by Viet Cong guerrillas at Bien Hoa, 20 miles north of Saigon; two Americans are killed.

1960

December 20	National Front for the Liberation of the South, commonly known as the National Liberation Front (NFL) is founded.

1963

November 2	President Ngo Dinh Diem is overthrown and killed in a military coup.

1964

August 2–4	Gulf of Tonkin incidents: attack on USS *Maddox* on August 2 and then attack on USS *Maddox* and USS *Turner Joy* on August 4.

1965

March 2	Operation Rolling Thunder begins.

Committee declaring that "the fundamental path of development for the revolution in South Vietnam is that of violent struggle [and that it was necessary] to use the strength of the masses ... in combination with military strength ... to overthrow the ruling power of the imperialist and feudalist forces."[6] In rapid order the National Front for the Liberation of the South or National Liberation Front (NFL) for short, was created in late 1960 as the umbrella organization for opposition to the Diem regime; while the NFL went about mobilizing the people and building its political infrastructure in the south, military cadres were formed into the People's Liberation Armed Forces (PLAF), soon to be better known as the Viet Cong. The core of the PLAF was built around an estimated 10,000 hardened Viet Minh guerrillas who remained in the south following the Geneva Accords.

For all his popularity with his American patrons as the counterweight to communist expansion and the appearance of control, President Diem and his family entourage had by 1963 alienated much of South Vietnamese society and pushed others into the arms of the NFL. In addition, Diem misjudged the political and socio-economic nature of revolutionary warfare, preferring to view the Viet Cong insurgency in narrow military terms, which was a view generally shared by his American advisers.[7] Even when Washington officials pushed Diem and his brother, Ngo Dinh Nhu, to enact democratic reforms they had little leverage. "They [Washington officials] knew what Diem knew: that the United States ... needed Diem at least as much as he needed the United States" and "in the perpetual contest of wills, between stopping American assistance or enacting comprehensive reforms, Diem easily won."[8] Nonetheless, the day of reckoning was fast approaching. On November 2, 1963 President Diem was overthrown by the South Vietnamese military in a coup that would leave him and his brother Nhu dead. It also would also unleash a period of protracted political instability in Saigon—one that would see five changes of leadership over the course of 18 months—even as the Viet Cong insurgency was intensifying across the country.

This was the volatile situation that President Lyndon Johnson and his new administration were grappling with at the beginning of August 1964 when a seemingly minor and inadvertent series of military encounters in the waters off the coast of North Vietnam became a defining watershed for an American escalation in a conflict that it had for so long sought to keep at arm's length.

Flashpoint: The Gulf of Tonkin Incidents
The Gulf of Tonkin is the northern arm of the South China Sea that is bound by the northern coast of Vietnam to the west and China to the north and east; the Chinese island of Hainan lies to its east. Since late 1962, the U.S. Navy had been conducting ongoing maritime intelligence collection and electronic surveillance against Chinese and North Vietnamese coastal radar sites from the international waters of the Gulf of Tonkin as part of its DeSoto patrols. In February 1964, President Johnson authorized support for a program of covert air and naval harassment operations against North Vietnam by South Vietnamese forces, known as Operation Plan 34A (OPLAN 34A). Although distinctly different operations, Hanoi increasingly came to see the DeSoto patrols and OPLAN 34A activities as interrelated, if not one and the same. On the night of July 30/31, 1964 a team of South Vietnamese naval commandos raided the islands of Hon Me and Hon Nieu off the central coast of North Vietnam as part of OPLAN 34A. It is believed that this raid precipitated the ensuing events.

A few days later on the afternoon of August 2, while conducting a DeSoto patrol approximately 25 miles off the coast of North Vietnam in the Gulf of Tonkin the

The U.S. destroyer, USS *Maddox*, would be involved in two incidents in the Gulf of Tonkin in early August 1964 that would serve as a catalyst for American entry into the war in Vietnam. (Photo U.S. Navy)

American destroyer the USS *Maddox* came under attack by three North Vietnamese patrol boats. One of the PT boats was able to get close enough to launch two torpedoes before it was heavily damaged by gunfire from the *Maddox*. The other two PT boats also suffered some damage in the ensuing, but brief firefight, while the *Maddox* suffered a single 14.5-mm-round hit.[9] Upon learning of the attack, four F-8 Crusader fighters from the nearby USS *Ticonderoga* were sent to assist the *Maddox*. The Crusaders strafed the fleeing patrol boats with 20-mm cannon and 5-inch Zuni rockets, sinking the previously damaged PT boat. The *Maddox* was shortly thereafter joined by the USS *Turner Joy* and then both destroyers retired to the east.

Things would be more confused on the night of August 4 when both the *Maddox* and the *Turner Joy* while on joint patrol would report coming under a second attack by multiple unidentified vessels. High seas and rain squalls, poor visibility, and radar problems, however, hampered accurately identifying the threat. Confusion reigned. Over the next three hours the *Maddox* and *Turner Joy* undertook evasive maneuvers, reported automatic-weapons fire, torpedo attacks, and numerous radar and surface contacts.[10] Commander James Stockdale, commanding officer of Fighter Squadron 51 (VF-51), arriving on the scene had a different assessment from the cockpit of his Crusader. Years later he wrote that "I had the best seat in the house ... and our destroyers were just shooting at phantom targets—there were no PT boats there ... there was nothing but black water and American firepower."[11]

Nonetheless, the stage was set for American retaliation. At just before midnight in Washington on August 4, President Johnson ordered retaliatory strikes against North Vietnam. "Air action is now in execution [against] North Viet-Nam ... Yet our response, for the present, will be limited and fitting. We still seek no wider war."[12] Operation Pierce

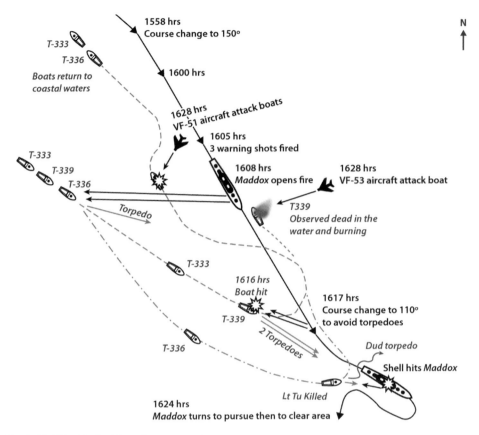

The Gulf of Tonkin incident, August 2, 1964.

Arrow called for naval aircraft strikes against four North Vietnamese patrol boat bases, as well as against the petroleum storage facility at Vinh. Over the course of the afternoon of August 5, 67 aircraft, including F-8 Crusaders, A-1 Skyraiders, and A-4 Skyhawks, launched from the decks of the USS *Ticonderoga* and the recently arrived USS *Constellation*.[13]

The Pierce Arrow reprisal attacks were considered a success. They sunk at least eight patrol boats and reportedly damaged another 21 boats and 90 percent of the petroleum storage facility at Vinh was reported destroyed.[14] The operation was not without cost. Lieutenant (j.g.) Everett Alvarez's Skyhawk was shot down over Hon Gai harbor and he was captured, becoming the first American prisoner of war and Lieutenant (j.g.) Richard Sather was killed when his Skyraider was hit by ground fire while attacking the naval base at Loc Ghao.[15] The attacks, however, clearly sent a strong message to Hanoi about American resolve. And to remove any doubts, the Pentagon announced the sending of additional reinforcements to the region, including the formation of an attack carrier group for the Western Pacific and the deployment of U.S. aircraft to South Vietnam and Thailand. Critically, on August 7, 1964 Congress authorized President Johnson "to take all necessary measures to repel any armed attack against the forces of the United States and to prevent further aggression."[16] There was now no turning back.

2. A GATHERING STORM

While the Pierce Arrow retaliatory strikes were considered a one-off event at the time, the strikes did open the door for a de facto policy of American military retaliation that would serve as the catalyst for implementing Operation Rolling Thunder seven months later. Although often viewed in hindsight as a foregone conclusion, the decision to embark on a sustained air campaign was the subject of intense and heated debated within the Johnson administration and among senior military officers from late 1964 onward; while there was a consensus over the need to be able to respond to future North Vietnamese and/or Viet Cong provocations, crucial questions over when, how, and where to do so were extremely contentious. Ultimately, a competing array of U.S. political, diplomatic, and military considerations ultimately influenced the formulation of a reprisal strategy, which was further affected by an ongoing leadership crisis in Saigon, a deteriorating situation on the battlefield in South Vietnam, and Cold War geo-strategic concerns.

The American Challenge

The autumn of 1964 found the Johnson administration grappling to advance an ambitious set of security and foreign policy objectives in Southeast Asia even as the situation was increasingly spinning out of control. As the de facto guarantor of South Vietnamese security the United States found itself in the unenviable position of trying to nurture the development of a democratic society and robust economy as a bulwark against communist aggression in the region, while in the midst of an ever-escalating guerrilla insurgency that was threatening the South's survival as a nation. The prospects were not good. Ten years of American security assistance, training, and equipment had failed to turn the tide on the battlefield or counter the Viet Cong's successful exploitation of popular resentment to repressive government policies. Moreover, Hanoi appeared firmly committed as ever to pump men and matériel southward as part of the war effort.

Against this increasingly desperate backdrop, the Johnson administration sought to advance four primary strategic objectives: 1) Strengthen the South Vietnamese government and provide it with a confidence boost; 2) Demonstrate American resolve and support for its South Vietnamese ally; 3) Deter Hanoi from actively directing and supporting

General William Westmoreland, as commander of American ground forces in South Vietnam, sought to fight a war of attrition against the Viet Cong and North Vietnamese forces arrayed against the Saigon government. The strategy, however, required an ever escalating number of troops at a time the Johnson administration sought to temper U.S. involvement.

Secretary of Defense McNamara was forced to deal with a revolving door of South Vietnamese military governments following the overthrow of the Diem regime in 1963.

the Viet Cong insurgency; and 4) Push the North Vietnamese leadership into negotiating a favorable settlement to the war in the south.

Continuing setbacks on the battlefield, an unwieldy and unresponsive chain of command, and personal rivalries within the senior officer corps greatly hindered the effectiveness of the South Vietnamese military throughout 1964. Likewise, political intrigue and maneuvering by both civilian and military leaders complicated Washington's efforts to establish some degree of political stability in Saigon, institute democratic reforms, and build popular support for the government. Clearly, more aggressive U.S. action was needed to boost Vietnamese morale, reverse—or at least halt—the deteriorating military situation, and rally support for the government of General Nguyen Khanh, who was showing some ability to unite feuding elements of the South Vietnamese political, military, and religious establishment.[1]

Despite private fears within the administration that the situation in South Vietnam was unraveling, walking away and abandoning its ally was simply not an option. Not only would any hint of weakness likely embolden the North Vietnamese and their Viet Cong surrogates, but the global prestige and credibility of the United States was on the line in the fight against international communism. The impact of the communists coming to power would be catastrophic not only in Asia but in the rest of the world, declared National Security Action Memorandum 288, "where the South Vietnam conflict is regard as a test case of U.S. capacity to help a nation to meet the Communist 'war of liberation'."[2]

While there was some recognition that the Viet Cong were tapping into longstanding popular resentment with the Saigon government, most American officials firmly

18

believed that the insurgency was centrally controlled and directed from Hanoi. Without extensive political and material support from the North, it was believed that the Viet Cong insurgency would eventually wither and die in the face of combined American and South Vietnamese efforts. Since militarily sealing South Vietnam's porous borders was not a realistic option (although efforts to interdict supply routes running through southern Laos by bombing were ongoing), the answer lay in persuading—or compelling—Hanoi to withdraw its support. And it was this latter point that would become a deeply contentious topic throughout the remainder of 1964 and early 1965 for the White House.

Ultimately, the long-term U.S. goal was to end the war and leave a stable and secure South Vietnamese regime in place. Various carrot and stick options were explored in 1964, including offering Hanoi a large economic assistance package, but there gradually developed a consensus within the administration that the North Vietnamese leadership would not willingly abandon its support for the Viet Cong. Thus, American officials increasingly came around to relying on the use military force as the only way to drive Hanoi to the negotiating table. It was, however, a delicate balancing act as Washington tried to walk a fine line of tempering American escalation against fears of being pulled further toward a full-scale war, one that might very well ensnare the Soviet Union and China.

Coercive Diplomacy vs. Military Strategy

As documented in the *Pentagon Papers*, the debate in Washington over various policy options during this time was extremely intense and often acrimonious. It highlighted competing perspectives and assumptions within the Johnson administration about the role and utility of force to achieve American objectives in Southeast Asia. In very simplistic terms, the debate over the future course of America's Vietnam policy pitted the proponents of a measured, coercive diplomacy strategy against those championing unleashing U.S. military might to compel Hanoi to bend to Washington's will or have North Vietnam face utter destruction. All the while the potential of the crisis in Vietnam developing into a major Cold War confrontation loomed ominously over the discussions.

Two important components helped frame the debate. First, there was a widely accepted requirement that the United States should avoid at all costs becoming entangled in a ground war in Vietnam. This had been a longstanding policy tenet across multiple U.S. administrations. Moreover, it was especially relevant in the midst of a heated presidential election where President Johnson was presenting himself as the voice of moderation against a bellicose and reckless Senator Barry Goldwater. For even a hint of a drift toward a land war would be politically dangerous for the administration. The second important component was the widely held belief, especially in U.S. military circles, in the ability of air power to be a decisive factor in defeating an enemy either on the battlefield or by forcing political capitulation. Even the existence of post-World War II studies questioning this assumption apparently did not dissuade senior American commanders. Thus, if air power was to be the tool of American escalation in achieving the Johnson administration's four strategic objectives in Vietnam, then the only real issue remaining was exactly how it was to be employed.

The approach favored by Secretary of Defense Robert McNamara and other senior White House advisers called for the tailored use of American air power in a flexible response to changing conditions. Through "carefully calculated doses of force," the United States could coerce Hanoi into modifying its behavior and pressure the North Vietnamese leadership into agreeing to negotiated end to the conflict.[3] This approach also met with Ambassador Maxwell Taylor's desire for a "tit for tat retaliation" that would send a strong signal of American resolve and boost South Vietnamese morale. Proponents also pointed out that such a strategy of limited air warfare would likely avoid drawing either the Soviet Union or China into the conflict.

A contrasting approach, however, called for the use of overwhelming force to ruthlessly punish Hanoi and cripple the North's ability to support the insurgency in the south. The Joint Chiefs of Staff in particular, believed that if the United States really wanted to affect Hanoi's behavior, it would have to "hit hard at its capabilities."[4] Accordingly, Admiral U.S. Grant Sharp as Commander-in-Chief Pacific recommended striking North Vietnamese lines of communications and infiltration routes into South Vietnam, as well as mining various ports and conducting an escalating series of air attacks against all military and industrial targets in North Vietnam.[5] Such actions, he believed would starkly demonstrate Washington's resolve and underscore Hanoi's vulnerability. General Curtis LeMay, U.S. Air Force Chief of Staff, was even more outspoken. If the North failed to stop its aggression, he said that the United States should be prepared "to bomb them back to the Stone Age."[6] Although not as prone to hyperbole as General LeMay, most senior American military officers were confident—perhaps too confident—that the North Vietnamese would be unable to stand up to an American air onslaught and would have little choice but to opt for a negotiated settlement to the conflict.

The White House policy debate came to a major turning point in early November 1964 when President Johnson formed an inter-agency working group of the National Security Council (NSC), headed by Assistant Secretary of State for Far Eastern Affairs William Bundy, "to conduct a thorough re-examination of our Vietnam policy and to present ... alternatives and recommendations as to our future course of action."[7] Although sharp differences existed between the two competing schools of thought over the use of force, there was strong agreement within the group that the current status quo was not working and something new needed to be done. Any new policy should also provide the President with a high degree of flexibility and not foreclose future options. Furthermore, there was an implicit bias within the group toward negotiating an end to the conflict, rather than in seeking military victory, much to

Admiral U.S. Grant Sharp, as Commander-in-Chief Pacific Command, was highly skeptical of White House efforts to fight a limited and restrictive air campaign, but nonetheless did his best to implement the strategy despite his misgivings. (Photo U.S. Navy)

the displeasure of senior military officers. Likewise, the Joint Chiefs of Staff thought intervention by China was unlikely[8] which was a stark contrast with the majority NSC viewpoint that Peking would "feel compelled" to assist Hanoi.[9] There was, nonetheless, a significant amount of give and take among the members so that a consensus was achieved, but only by the "process of compromising alternatives into the lowest common denominator [and] thereby precluding any real Presidential choice among viable options."[10] And this would have profound consequences down the road for the conduct of what was to become Operation Rolling Thunder.

Bundy's NSC working group recommended a two-phase plan for the use of American air power to Johnson. Phase 1 would be an extension of the current actions with some increased air activity in Laos and tit for tat reprisals to Viet Cong attacks on U.S. forces. Phase 2 called for a campaign of gradually escalating air strikes against the North. The President approved Phase 1 in early December. He also gave his approval in principle for Phase

As Chief of Staff of Air Force (1961–65), General Curtis LeMay advocated the unbridled use of air power against North Vietnam to counter its aggression in the South. (Photo U.S. Air Force)

2, but was apparently reluctant to grant final authorization until he felt it was absolute necessary and unavoidable.[11] Thus, by the end of 1964 the United States was clearly on course for an expanded military role in Vietnam.

Flaming Dart: The Prequel

Although the United States was clearly moving toward greater military escalation in Vietnam, the complex and highly volatile political situation in Saigon presented significant obstacles to the NSC plan. Ambassador Taylor had orders from Johnson to aggressively push the Saigon regime to make substantial progress on political and military reforms before the United States would move forward on Phase 2 escalation. Unfortunately, Taylor quickly found himself caught up in the internal South Vietnamese political crisis. Throughout December and into late January 1965 the country witnessed government purges, successive military interventions, and Buddhist rioting that became increasingly anti-American. A one point it appeared that Ambassador Taylor was about to be declared persona non grata and expelled from the country. All this threatened to poison U.S.–South Vietnamese relations, but both sides eventually realized they had little choice but to seek accommodation.

In the meantime the insurgency continued unabated as the Viet Cong took advantage of the ongoing chaos. In late December, for instance, two Viet Cong regiments overran a government garrison at Binh Gia, just east of Saigon. An ill-coordinated effort to retake the position ended in disaster with several South Vietnamese battalions being decimated along with the loss of at least nine helicopters.[12] In addition, the Viet Cong were showing an increased willingness to target Americans. On Christmas Eve 1964,

Viet Cong infiltrators blew up the Brinks Hotel in Saigon, which was housing U.S. military personnel. Two American officers were killed and another 58 Americans were injured in the explosion.[13]

None of this, however, elicited the American reprisal response as called for in Phase 1. Apparently there was concern in Washington that the United States would appear to be trying to fight its way out of the domestic crisis in South Vietnam without having first secured the long-term reforms it believed necessary to stabilize the situation there. In light of the deteriorating military and political conditions in early 1965, even William Bundy recommended that the United States initiate some limited reprisal measures to strengthen Washington's hand. The Joint Chiefs went further in late January with their dire warning that "the next significant provocation be met with positive, timely, and appropriate response (preferably within 24 hours) against selected targets in North Vietnam" and noted that contingency plans had been made under the name of Operation Flaming Dart.[14]

Just after midnight on February 7, 1965, the Viet Cong launched two dramatic attacks against U.S. military personnel in the central highlands. First Viet Cong guerrillas struck an American Military Advisory Command Vietnam (MACV) compound north of Pleiku with small arms and satchel charges, damaging several buildings, killing one American,

On Christmas Eve 1964, Viet Cong infiltrators blew up the Brinks Hotel in Saigon, which was housing U.S. military personnel; two American died in the explosion and another 58 were injured.

Just after midnight on February 7, 1965, Viet Cong sappers infiltrated Camp Holloway near Pleiku and were able to destroy five helicopters and damaged another 17 aircraft belonging to the U.S. Army's 52nd Aviation Battalion. President Johnson ordered Operation Flaming Dart reprisal attacks against the North in response.

and wounding two dozen more. Almost simultaneously Viet Cong sappers infiltrated nearby Camp Holloway, headquarters of the U.S. Army's 52nd Aviation Battalion. A series of explosions left five helicopters in ruins, damaged another eleven, and left a further six fixed-winged aircraft seriously damaged. Accompanying mortar fire then struck the American barracks, producing heavy casualties. In the end, the two attacks left eight American dead and 128 wounded.[15]

Enough was enough for President Johnson. "They are killing our men while they sleep," Johnson fumed, and "we have kept our guns over the mantle ... for a long time with little to show for our restraint."[16] With both Taylor and Westmoreland calling for an immediate response and support from the rest of his national security team, Johnson ordered retaliatory air strikes to be undertaken immediately. Four pre-selected targets in the southern part of North Vietnam were picked by Johnson: North Vietnamese army barracks at Chap Le, Vit Thu Lu, Dong Hoi and Vu Con and were to be struck by U.S. Air Force and Navy aircraft along with participation from the Vietnamese National Air Force (VNAF) as a show of unity.[17] By the early afternoon of February 7 the first wave of aircraft was airborne and heading toward their targets.

Unfortunately, deteriorating weather conditions as a result of the annual northeast monsoon season obscured three of the four targets and only naval aircraft from the USS *Coral Sea* and USS *Hancock* were able to carry out the attack on Dong Hoi barracks complex as planned. The other missions were aborted. The following day, military commanders urged Johnson to continue the strikes given the inability to attack all the targets the previous day, but the President's NSC advisers felt that a second strike

The flamboyant chief of the South Vietnamese Air Force, General Nguyen Cao Ky (center), often personally led airstrikes against North Vietnamese targets in the early months of the air campaign. His political maneuvering and corrupt reputation, however, caused constant headaches for his American allies. (Photo National Museum of the U.S. Air Force)

"might give Hanoi and Moscow the impression that we [the United States] had begun a sustained air offensive."[18] And the President agreed. However, at the urging of Taylor and Westmoreland authorization was given for the VNAF to strike its original target at Vu Con. Accordingly on the afternoon of February 8 a flight of 24 VNAF A-1 Skyraiders led by Air Vice-Marshal Nguyen Cao Key, along with a U.S. Air Force escort, flew north from Da Nang to attack Chap Le, just north of the DMZ, Vu Con having once again being obscured by bad weather. Confusion reigned over the target as Vietnamese and American planes attempted to coordinate the assault in the face of strong enemy anti-aircraft fire and ultimately only light damage was done to the facility.[19] Nonetheless, the first VNAF air strike north of the DMZ was considered a success.

Condemnation from North Vietnam and its communist allies was swift and defiant. Hanoi called the attacks "a new and utterly grave act of war," while protest marches against American aggression took place in Moscow and Peking as both countries pledged their continued support and assistance to North Vietnam. Radio Hanoi also called for the Viet Cong to increase their efforts and a few days later they did exactly that. On February 10, Viet Cong operatives smuggled suitcases containing an estimated

100 pounds of explosives into the Viet Cuong Hotel in Qui Nhon. The ensuing explosion leveled the building, which housed U.S. military personnel, leaving 23 Americans and seven Vietnamese dead and dozens injured.

In response, President Johnson ordered Flaming Dart II the next day with U.S. Navy and VNAF aircraft delivering the retaliation. Nearly 100 aircraft from the carriers *Coral Sea*, *Hancock*, and *Ranger* attacked the Chanh Hoa barracks complex, just north of Dong Hoi, and 28 VNAF Skyraiders supported by U.S. Air Force F-100s restruck Chap Le. Heavy defensive fire, bad weather, and poor visibility resulted in only light to moderate damage to both targets. The Navy lost three planes that day to enemy ground fire, while nearly two-thirds of the VNAF Skyraiders suffered significant battle damage.[20] One of the Navy planes lost was an F-8D Crusader piloted by Lieutenant Commander Robert Shumaker of Fighter Squadron 154 (VF-154). Shumaker was quickly captured after ejecting and taken to Hanoi's central prison complex, Hao Lo, but better known to the American POWs as the "Hanoi Hilton," where he joined Everett Alvarez.[21]

The Die is Cast

The Flaming Dart air strikes of February 7–11 were intend to send a very clear, yet measured message to Hanoi about American resolve and the Washington's growing impatience with the rising Viet Cong activity that the North Vietnamese were fueling. As such, the attacks were not the punitive retaliation designed to punish Hanoi that American military commanders were seeking, but rather signaled the opening round in Washington's coercive diplomacy strategy. For earlier in the month, Special Assistant for National Security Affairs McGeorge Bundy (brother of William) headed a fact finding mission to Saigon at President Johnson's behest to assess policy options for the way forward. Central to their findings was the belief that a "policy of graduated and continuing reprisal ... is the most promising course available."[22] It was to be the stick of military pressure in the administration's carrot and stick approach, but one that was judiciously applied. "The objective is not to 'win' an air war against Hanoi, but to influence the course of the struggle in the South"[23] and weaken Hanoi's resolve to support the Viet Cong insurgency. Reprisals would be reduced or stopped if and when Viet Cong activity was reduced or stopped. Importantly, McGeorge Bundy and his team rejected the Joint Chiefs' desire to launch a swift and massive aerial assault, which they believed could send the conflict spinning out of control. On February 13, after meeting with his advisers, President Johnson approved "a program of measured and limited air action ... until further notice" against "selected targets" in North Vietnam.[24] This air campaign was to be called Operation Rolling Thunder.

The strategy was not without its critics. As Admiral Sharp cautioned the Joint Chiefs in a February 17 memo that "While it may be politically desirable to speak publicly in terms of a 'graduated reprisal' program, I would hope that we are thinking, and will act, in terms of a 'graduated pressures' philosophy which has more of a connotation of steady, relentless movement toward our objective of convincing Hanoi and Peking of the prohibitive cost to them of their program of subversion, insurgency and aggression in Southeast Asia. We must be certain that we are dealing from a posture of strength before we sit down at the bargaining table. [Furthermore] any political program which is designed to formulate terms and procedures for reaching agreement on cessation of a graduated military pressures program will be successful in proportion to the effectiveness of the military pressures program itself."[25]

NVA regulars at Dien Bien Phu in 1954. Within a decade they would be pitted against the might of the United Sates.

Other senior military commanders shared Sharp's concerns too, fearful that the administration's approach was seriously miscalculating what a politically subservient military campaign could accomplish. To them this new course of action was far too constrained and too weak an approach for the task at hand. Ultimately they would be proven right.

In the meantime, however, it was aye aye sir and planning for this new phase of the air war began to move forward in earnest. U.S. men and equipment needed to be prepared, ships and planes moved into position, logistics set up, targets identified and selected, and coordination and liaison arrangements with allies put into place. Everything needed to be ready and in place by February 20, the planned start of Operation Rolling Thunder. After nearly a year of debate and failed efforts to stabilize the political and military situation in South Vietnam, the United States was ready to flex its military might directly against North Vietnam in the hope of turning the tide in its favor.

3. THE AIR CAMPAIGN UNFOLDS

In what was to become the largest and longest sustained air campaign in U.S. history up to that time, Operation Rolling Thunder started off poorly. The first mission scheduled for February 20, 1965 was scratched as a result of the South Vietnamese military's preoccupation with coup concerns and the ongoing political instability. The next three planned missions, likewise, fell victim to political intrigue and bad weather conditions. It would be a full 17 days following President Johnson's go ahead that the air campaign would actually begin. Even then the initial air strikes failed to send the meaningful message of strength and resolve that Washington had intended, or upon whom the ultimate success of the campaign depended.

What had originally been envisioned as an eight-week campaign of coercive diplomacy would eventually stretch into an astonishing 180 weeks—more than three and half years—with American pilots dropping more bombs on North Vietnam than were dropped on all of Europe during World War II. In the end, however, conflicting and often competing military and political strategies would doom it to failure as it fell well short of achieving its primary objective of bringing a negotiated end to the war in South Vietnam. More important, the war and America's role in Vietnam would expand to unprecedented levels during the course of the air campaign, dragging the United States ever deeper into a ground war it sought so desperately to avoid. It would take another four years—and another bombing campaign—after the end of Rolling Thunder before Washington and Hanoi were able to finally reached a negotiated a peace settlement.

The Opening Salvo

The first Rolling Thunder mission, a joint American–South Vietnamese effort, finally got underway on the afternoon of March 2, 1965—six days before the first of 3,500 U.S. Marines would wade ashore at Da Nang—signaling the start of the planned eight-week air campaign. Rolling Thunder 5 (Rolling Thunder 1–4 having been cancelled) called for attacks on the ammunition storage depot at Xom Bang and the naval base at Quang Khe, all in the southern panhandle of North Vietnam. In keeping with President Johnson's desire for joint action, the U.S. Air Force was to strike Xom Bang, while the VNAF with the Air Force flying cover was to hit Quang Khe.

Although the targets were of relatively minimal military importance, the forces arrayed for this first opening salvo of the air campaign were indeed impressive. Launching from bases in South Vietnam and Thailand for the assault on Xom Bang, 35 miles north of the DMZ, the American strike force consisted of 44 F-105 Thunderchiefs, 40 F-100 Super Sabres, and 20 B-57 Canberra bombers, along with six KC-135 tankers for inflight refueling and two RF-101 Voodoo reconnaissance aircraft for battle-damage assessment. A planned inclusion of B-52 heavy bombers out of Guam in the attack force was canceled at the last minute for fear by White House officials that such an all-out aerial onslaught might well trigger direct Chinese or Soviet intervention. Simultaneously, a flight of 19 VNAF A-1 Skyraiders took off from Da Nang, accompanied by nearly 60 U.S. Air Force F-105s and F-100s, for the attack on Quang Khe, about 65 miles north of the DMZ.

Rushed over to South Vietnam in the run-up to the air campaign, the F-100 Super Sabre was forced into action as a close air support and flak suppression aircraft, a mission it was ill-suited to perform. Over time the F-100 squadrons steadily gave way to the more capable F-105s.
(Photo National Museum of the U.S. Air Force)

Operating first out of South Vietnamese and later Thai air bases, the F-105D Thunderchief or "Thud," loaded here with M117 750-pound general purpose bombs became the primary Air Force attack aircraft over the North. (Photo U.S. Air Force)

Xom Bang was hit first. Waves of F-100s were swarming over the target area pummeling enemy anti-aircraft positions with rockets and 20-mm cannon fire as the first wave of F-105s armed with 250-pound and 500-pound bombs led by Lieutenant Colonel Robinson "Robbie" Risner arrived on the scene. Rolling unto the target, the attacking aircraft faced intense ground fire. A supporting Super Sabre burst into flames as did a Thunderchief on its bombing run. Both pilots ejected safely. Captain Robert Baird was picked up by an air force helicopter—the first combat rescue in North Vietnam—but 1st Lieutenant Hayden Lockhart was captured after having evaded for nearly a week, becoming the first Air Force prisoner of war. Even before Risner's strike was completed the second wave of F-105s arrived prematurely, forcing the planes to circle the target and creating inviting targets for the North Vietnamese gunners below. Confusion reigned as the American planes, now including the B-57 bombers, pressed their attack. When it was finally over, Xom Bang was a smoldering wreck and being rocked by secondary explosions under the weight of 120 tons of American ordnance.[1]

Meanwhile some 30 miles to the northeast, Quang Khe was under air assault by 19 VNAF A-1 Skyraiders loaded with 500-pound bombs and cluster munitions. The Skyraiders were accompanied by nearly 60 F-100s and F-105s flying escort and providing flak suppression. Dropping 20 tons of munitions on the naval base and adjacent facilities the South Vietnamese strike destroyed or heavily damaged numerous buildings, including repair shops and supply warehouses.[2] Three patrol boats caught at their berths were also reported sunk. One F-100D was shot down during the attack, but the pilot rescued and a VNAF A-1 suffered critical damage and was later written off.

U.S. officials in Saigon claimed the air strikes destroyed or heavily damaged 75–80 percent of both targets and the attackers had faced only "light and not accurate" ground fire.[3] Lieutenant Colonel Risner would disagree with the latter statement. The loss of three F-105Ds and two F-100Ds to enemy fire and the capture of one of its pilots made the missions costly and it was apparent that American pilots were facing a steep learning curve.

A cumbersome White House targeting process, coordination problems with the VNAF, and continuing poor weather delayed the next Rolling Thunder mission by nearly two weeks. Rolling Thunder 6 called for the VNAF to strike the North Vietnamese military complex on Hon Goi or Tiger Island, some 20 miles off the coast from Vinh city, along with a joint Air Force–Navy strike against the Phu Qui ammunition depot about 100 miles southwest of Hanoi. The VNAF attack on Tiger Island took place on March 14 when 24 A-1s armed with 250-pound, 500-pound, and 750-pound bombs and 2.75-inch rockets stuck the facility. Once again, F-100s and F-105s provided flak suppression and air cover. The facility suffered light to moderate damage and all planes returned safely to base. The next day with improving weather, a massive 137-plane American strike force hit the Phu Qui ammunition depot. Air Force F-105s and Navy A-1s and A-4s dropped 250-pound and 750-pound bombs and rocketed the target area with 2.75-inch rockets; napalm was also used for the first time against a North Vietnamese target.[4] Post-strike reconnaissance indicated that about 33 percent of the target area was hit with four buildings completely destroyed and another 17 severely damaged.[5] No American aircraft were lost over the target, but one Skyraider returning to the USS *Ranger* crashed into the sea, killing the pilot.

Despite the grandiose announcements of success, frustration among civilian and military officials with the slow pace and limited impact of air campaign was building. The air strikes had apparently done nothing to dissuade Hanoi from supporting the Viet Cong or pushing it closer to the negotiating table and the situation on the battlefield in South Vietnam remained critical. "It appears ... evident that to date [North Vietnamese] leaders believe air strikes at present levels on their territory are meaningless," wrote Ambassador Taylor in March, and "I fear that to date Rolling Thunder in their eyes has been merely a few isolated thunder claps."[6] Thus the urgent need, he argued, for an increased tempo and intensity to convince Hanoi of progressively severe punishment if it failed to change its behavior. Moreover, both Taylor and General Westmoreland, pushed for a several-week program of strikes relentlessly marching north of the 19th parallel toward Hanoi itself to remove any doubt as to American resolve.[7]

American military commanders back in Washington were advocating for changes in the air campaign too. A mid-March report by Army Chief of Staff General Harold Johnson to the Joint Chiefs and Secretary McNamara following a visit to Saigon called for a 21-point program of initiatives to better accomplish American objectives in Vietnam. With respect to Rolling Thunder, General Johnson's report called for an increase in the scope and tempo of the strikes and a removal of many of the self-imposed restrictions on the use of American air power in the north.[8] Shortly thereafter, new presidential guidelines were formulated that were designed to transform Rolling Thunder from a sporadic, halting effort into a regularized and sustained bombing effort. Accordingly, future strikes were to be packaged into a weekly program, the precise timing of the strikes would be left up to field commanders, and the requirement for simultaneous U.S.–VNAF strikes was

F-105Ds flying a mission strike profile into North Vietnam.
(Photo National Museum of the U.S. Air Force)

The venerable A-1 Skyraider proved to be one of the U.S. Navy's most capable and versatile aircraft in the early years of the war by functioning as an attack bomber, provider of close air support and flak suppression, and as a combat air patrol rescue aircraft. (Photo Emil Buehler Library, National Naval Aviation Museum)

dropped. In addition, strikes would no longer to be tied to specific Viet Cong attacks or actions in South Vietnam, but were part and parcel of the wider air war against the North.[9]

While these changes were certainly welcomed, the White House still continued to maintain strict control over targeting decisions and the new operational changes still fell far short of what most military commanders thought was necessary to achieve American objectives. For instance, the instituting of armed reconnaissance missions— whereby aircraft overflew designated transportation route segments with the authority to attack trucks, trains, or watercraft—was designed to disrupt the flow of supplies southward. However, these "armed recce" missions (as they came to be known) were few and far between; only three per week starting with Rolling Thunder 7. This led Admiral Sharp to remark that "the North Vietnamese probably didn't even know the planes were there!"[10] Likewise, an ambitious and aggressive proposal to systematically degrade Hanoi's lines of communication and infiltration routes to the south was meant with resistance from Secretary McNamara, who wanted a scaled-down and more restrained version. As a result the guidelines for the new interdiction program constrained the Joint Chiefs "from putting forth a proposal they considered adequate or forceful enough to do the job."[11]

There were, however, some concessions to military commanders' concerns. As the air campaign began to evolve in mid-March, White House authorization was granted for a major effort to take out the North Vietnamese radar tracking and warning network, to launch attacks on key bridges south of the 20th parallel as part of the new interdiction effort, to conduct low-level pre- and post-strike reconnaissance, and to dramatically increase the number of armed reconnaissance missions. Nonetheless, a failure to commit to any fixed timetable, extensive restrictions on targets north of the 21st parallel, the unwillingness to

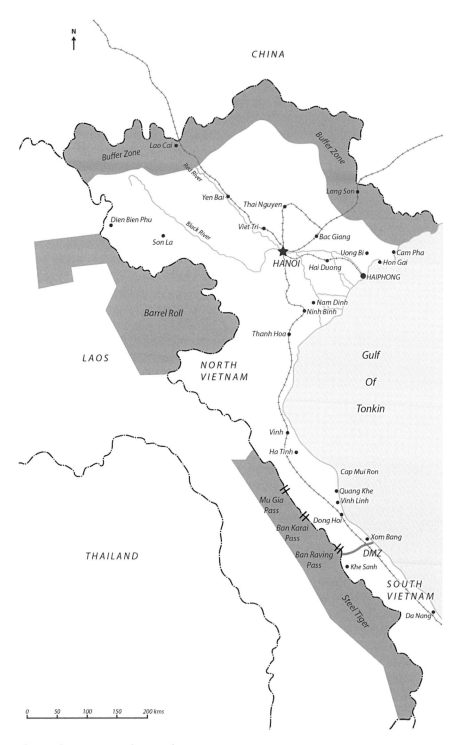

The North Vietnamese theater of operations.

strike MiG fighter bases near Hanoi, and the rejection of aerial mining of North Vietnamese ports hindered commanders' efforts to prosecute the air war and raised the frustration level among pilots flying Rolling Thunder missions. Moreover, the political necessity of being able to modulate the pace and tempo of the air campaign as a prerequisite of the coercive diplomacy strategy complicated long-term military planning and diminished the ability to apply steadily increasing military pressure on Hanoi. Coercion, not subjugation, remained the defining principle of Rolling Thunder for the time being.

Op Tempo Rises

Despite Johnson's and McNamara's desire to tightly control the bombing, the air war was indeed heating up. From mid-March to mid-April the operation tempo of Rolling Thunder rose significantly as the air campaign gained pace. Starting on March 22 a combined force of the Air Force, Navy, and VNAF undertook a series of "radar busting" missions to at least cripple, if not destroy, nine heavily defended North Vietnamese radar sites south of the 20th parallel. Over the course of the next ten days American and South Vietnamese aircraft pounded sites from Dong Hoi to Ha Tinh and north of Vinh, as well as those on the offshore islands of Hon Matt, Hon Ngu, and Bach Long Vi, with varying degrees of success. The intense hail of anti-aircraft fire from the well-defended sites resulted in the loss of nine American planes and the death of two pilots.

The USS *Sacramento* (center) refueling the aircraft carrier USS *Hancock* and destroyer USS *Robison* in the Gulf of Tonkin, 1965.

A-4 Skyhawk preparing to launch off the USS *Hancock* in the opening round of Rolling Thunder, March 1965. (Photo U.S. Navy)

On one such mission on March 26, a 70-plane strike force from the USS *Hancock*'s Carrier Wing 21 (CVW-21) was charged with taking out the radar site at Ha Tinh, southeast of Vinh city. While the A-4 Skyhawks made bombing runs on the radar facility, the A-1 Skyraiders and F-8 Crusaders hammered the air defenses with bombs, rockets, and 20-mm cannon fire. During his sixth pass over the target, Lieutenant (j.g.) Gus Gudmunson's A-1H was severely damaged by 37-mm anti-aircraft fire. "I should have stopped after the fourth pass ... but we were too stupid and gung ho to know better," recalls Gudmunson.[12] Turning toward the ocean, he coaxed his crippled plane southward toward Da Nang to make an emergency landing. He walked away from the crash landing, but the aircraft was written off as a total loss.

The radar-busting missions were a baptism of fire for most young pilots, but skill and luck often weren't enough for even experienced pilots. During an earlier March 22 bombing of the Vinh Son radar facility by eight Air Force F-105s, the flight's lead aircraft was crippled by anti-aircraft fire, forcing Lieutenant Colonel Risner—commanding officer of the 67th Tactical Fighter Squadron (TFS) and of Xom Bang fame—to eject. Fortunately, he was quickly rescued by an Air Force amphibious flying boat and returned to his squadron in Thailand. Less than two weeks later Risner would be back in the thick of things once again.

Finally given the green light to go after the North Vietnamese lines of communication and infiltration routes to the south, Admiral Sharp began to target key bridges south of the 20th parallel in early April as part of Rolling Thunder 9. Three major highway–rail-road bridges were to be struck in the initial wave of attacks: the bridge at Dong Phuong

Thuong by the Navy and the bridge at Thanh Hoa by the Air Force on April 3, while the VNAF would strike Dong Hoi bridge the following day. All the targets were considered critical parts of the North Vietnamese supply pipeline to the south and their destruction would be a significant milestone for the budding American interdiction effort. But it would not be easy; even more difficult in one instance than anyone could have foreseen at the time.

First up were the Dong Phuong Thuong and Thanh Hoa bridges. Located some 100 miles south of Hanoi, the recently rebuilt 540-foot-long-span Thanh Hoa bridge— known locally as "The Dragon's Jaw"—had been personally dedicated by Ho Chi Minh in 1964 and carried nearly 3,000 tons of vehicular and rail traffic across the Song Ma River each day.[13] Located some 12 miles to the north of the Thanh Hoa bridge and also along national Route 1 was the equally important Dong Phuong Thuong bridge that spanned the Song Len River. The Navy struck first on April 3 when aircraft from the *Hancock* rolled onto the target. In the first wave 35 A-4 dropped everything from 250-pound to 1,000-pound bombs on the bridge and its approaches, while supporting 16 F-8s let loose a steady stream of 2.75-inch rocket and 20-mm cannon fire on the enemy defensive positions. A second wave from the USS *Coral Sea* soon followed, likewise pounding the target. When it was all over the 99-plane strike had delivered more than 72 tons of munitions on the target, dropping the center span of the bridge, heavily damaging the northern span, and leaving the road and rail approaches cratered and unserviceable.[14] One of CVW-21's A-4C Skyhawks was shot down and the pilot, Lieutenant Commander Raymond Vohden, captured.

Later that afternoon the Air Force flew into the teeth of The Dragon's Jaw defenses when 53 planes of the 67th TFS and the 613th TFS struck the Thanh Hoa Bridge. Once again the Korean War ace, Lieutenant Colonel Risner, led 31 F-105s on their missile and bombing runs against the bridge, while another 15 F-105s and seven F-100s struck enemy anti-aircraft positions. Supporting the mission were an additional 26 aircraft, including KC-130 tankers, 12 F-100s flying combat air patrol and rescue cover, and RF-101s for pre- and post-strike photo reconnaissance. Even before the flak suppression strikes were finished Risner and 15 other Thunderchiefs armed with two AGM-12 Bullpup missiles began their runs on the bridge, aiming for critical weak points on the center span. On their second go—each missile had to be manually guided to the target—it became apparent that hits on the bridge by 250-pound warheads were having little effect; "as effective as shooting BB pellets at a Sherman tank."[15] The second wave of F 105s dropping 45 tons of 750-pound bombs on the bridge's end spans likewise inflicted only negligible damage.[16] As the Air Force planes departed the scene—less one F-100D and one RF-101C brought down by anti-aircraft fire—smoke bellowed from the target area, but the Dragon's Jaw remained defiantly intact.

A follow-up attack the next day by 48 F-105s armed with 750-pound bombs and supported by 21 F-100s had somewhat better success in damaging the bridge with 112 tons of bombs, but still failed to knock the bridge down.[17] Once again the indomitable Robbie Risner would direct this strike and be awarded the first Air Force Cross of the war for his actions over Thanh Hoa those two days in April. The second attack was overshadowed, however, by the surprise appearance of four North Vietnamese MiG-17 fighters conducting a quick hit and run attack that successfully downed two bomb-laden F-105Ds. (A similar attack the day before during the Navy's strike on the Dong Phuong

Thuong bridge damaged an F-8E.) In addition, another F-105D was lost to enemy anti-aircraft fire and the pilot, Captain Carlyle "Smitty" Harris, was captured.[18] An Air Force A-1H flying rescue cover and searching for downed airmen from the previous day's attack was also lost on the 4th and the pilot killed. And this was just the opening round. In an epic test of wills the Dragon's Jaw would eventually be destroyed, but it would take another seven years and more than 800 sorties to finish the task.

Meanwhile, some 150 miles to the south the South Vietnamese were attacking the Dong Hoi bridge. With the support of 14 Air Force planes, 20 VNAF Skyraiders armed primarily with 250-pound and 500-pound bombs struck the 400-foot wooden bridge over the Song Nhat Le River with more than 45 tons of munitions. Two spans of the bridge were dropped and three more heavily damaged, while both the southern and northern causeway approaches were reportedly cratered.[19] One VNAF Skyraider was shot down during the attack.

The initial bridge attacks of early April had been costly, but provided some valuable lessons in the school of hard knocks. A total of six American and two South Vietnamese planes had been lost, four U.S. pilots killed, and three more captured. Numerous aircraft suffered light to moderate damage from anti-aircraft fire. Underestimating the North Vietnamese air defenses—both on the ground and in the air—had cost the Americans planes and pilots. So too had their predictability in mounting follow-up strikes. As Captain Smitty Harris recalled following his release in 1973, "We came in the same route, the same altitude, [and] same tactics [on the second day at Thanh Hoa]. They could have looked at their watches and started shooting."[20] It also wasn't enough to simply disable or damage a bridge once, as the North Vietnamese proved extremely adept at quickly repairing most damage or finding creative alternatives to bridge rivers. Thus, many targets required repeated attacks—as the Dragon's Jaw would harshly demonstrate—and North Vietnamese gunners quickly learned to unleash everything they had into the air above the bridge, knowing full well that American planes had to fly through the barrage on their

Colonel Robinson Risner was a Korean War veteran pilot and one of the most decorated Air Force pilots of his era. As commander of the 67th TFS he would lead the first Rolling Thunder strikes against Xom Bang, North Vietnam on March 2, 1965. He would be shot down twice in 1965, the latter time leading to his capture and imprisonment in the infamous Hanoi Hilton. He was released in February 1973 and rose to the rank of brigadier general.

RF-101C Voodoo reconnaissance aircraft from 20th TRS based in Ubon, Thailand. (Photo U.S. Air Force)

bombing runs to be effective. It was likened to flying through an "exploding curtain of steel" by one pilot.[21]

Nonetheless by the end of April the interdiction effort south of the 20th parallel was showing some signs of success. Of the 27 bridges targeted, 26 had been destroyed or knocked out of service, along with seven ferries. Vastly increased armed recce missions— up from three sorties per day to 24 per day—had largely immobilized daytime road and rail traffic along the southern panhandle's main transportation arteries and leaving in their wake burnt-out trucks, destroyed locomotives and boxcars, and sunken watercraft of all sizes. With the removal of altitude restrictions on reconnaissance flights and the arrival of the first four (of eventually 12) RF-101C Voodoos of the 15th Tactical Reconnaissance Squadron (TRS) at Udorn, Thailand, by the end of March, regular aerial coverage of the north under Operation Blue Tree improved dramatically.[22] The Air Force's 2nd Air Division in Thailand, under the command of Lieutenant General Joseph Moore, would also be augmented with several EB-66 electronic warfare aircraft to provide electronic countermeasure capability against Hanoi's air defenses.

A Problematic Juggling Act

Just as the air campaign was showing promise thanks to growing combat experience and some loosening of bombing restrictions, a series of crucial decisions by the Johnson administration concerning the future of U.S. military engagement in Vietnam and of the application of coercive diplomacy would ominously alter the course and impact of Operation Rolling Thunder.

Looming over every policy decision by the Johnson administration concerning the role and scope of American involvement in Vietnam was the foreboding specter of the war expanding outside the South and one that might draw in Hanoi's chief communist allies—the Soviet Union and China. This had the potential for not only dangerously escalating the war in Southeast Asia, but also of triggering a Cold War conflict on a global scale. At the same time, the United States needed to avoid being seen as too weak in its response and lacking the resolve to fully contest North Vietnamese aggression. Thus, there was the need for Washington to delicately calibrate and apply just the right amount of military force to push Ho Chi Minh to the negotiating table. In retrospect, it was a balancing act that was all but impossible to accomplish.

It was because of these overriding political concerns that the Johnson White House put in place an elaborate and painstakingly detailed set of rules of engagement and a complex targeting process for bombing the North. Although well-meaning, the end result was to greatly constrain and place strict limits on the use of American military force, which clearly undermined the effectiveness of the bombing campaign and sowed the seeds of failure for Rolling Thunder. Push-back by military commanders did result in some concessions over time, but the underlying strategic policy guidance rooted in gradual, escalating pressure and coercive diplomacy remained in place through the entire air campaign.

The military consequences for the execution of Rolling Thunder were telling and immediate. Tactical commanders and pilots flying missions found themselves coping a long list of requirements and restrictions that were frustrating and often nonsensical to the task at hand. The creation of a 30-mile no-fly buffer zone along the Chinese border, prohibiting attacks on "non-threatening" air defenses or those under construction, forbidding strikes against enemy aircraft on the ground, and a ban on returning fire against "neutral" Soviet and Chinese shipping in North Vietnamese ports were designed to avoid escalating the war, but they undercut military effectiveness and placed pilots and air crews at greater risk. Likewise, because Washington did not want to be seen as waging an all-out war of destruction against the North Vietnamese people extensive efforts were made to minimize civilian deaths and damage to civilian property. The most extreme and pronounced example of this was the imposition of prohibited (off limits completely) and restricted (required special Joint Chiefs approval) zones around Hanoi and Haiphong where dozens of key military targets and installations resided. Not surprisingly, the North Vietnamese quickly learned to locate military positions or equipment throughout the country in or near population centers or close to sensitive civilian buildings, like schools or hospitals, knowing full well the Americans would refrain from bombing them. Bombs, however, did go astray and civilian buildings were inevitably hit and North Vietnamese civilians were killed in the attacks, but nowhere close to the scale of civilian death and destruction of previous wars' bombing campaigns.

Even prior to the start of Rolling Thunder, however, political considerations trumped military strategy. It was the message that was of import, rather than the military value of the target being hit. This fundamental policy principle made Rolling Thunder one of the most micro-managed air campaigns in American history. Proposed targeting lists were forwarded from the Joint Chiefs to Secretary McNamara and the Department of State for vetting—some targets were removed and others added—before being submitted to the White House for approval. President Johnson would then personally select targets at his weekly Tuesday lunch with McNamara, often dictating the specific day and time for attacks, the number and types of planes, and the ordnance to be used.[23] Johnson had such firm control over the day-to-day operations that he once boasted, "I won't let those air force generals bomb the smallest outhouse ... with[out] checking with me."[24] While extremely frustrating for military planners and those seeking to maximize the use of

American air power, Johnson's approach reflected his faith in the highly surgical and controlled use of the air campaign to put just the right amount of pressure on Hanoi. "By keeping a lid on all the designated targets, I knew I could keep control of the war in my own hands," said the President. "But this control ... would be lost the moment we unleashed a total assault on the North" and in typical homespun Johnson fashion, he equated the bombing of the North in terms of a seduction rather than a rape: seduction was controllable and could be tempered according to the response.[25] Thus, the bombing could be increased or decreased according to Hanoi's willingness to negotiate.

The first opportunity to test this belief came when the White House announced a bombing halt beginning on May 13. It also followed growing international and domestic criticism of the bombing and an earlier public effort to woo the North Vietnamese leadership. (In April, Johnson publicly extended an offer of $1 billion in American economic development assistance if Hanoi would agree to end its aggression in the South.) By using this carrot and stick approach, Washington hoped to push Hanoi toward a negotiated end to the conflict. The attempt fell flat. Ho Chi Minh's resolve to support the Viet Cong insurgency remained as steadfast as ever. The increased air activity, reaching 4,000 sorties in May, was more of an inconvenience than a crippling blow to Hanoi's war effort as key military and economic infrastructure north of the 20th parallel remained untouched. Moreover, in the eyes of the North Vietnamese leadership the conflict was just beginning; they had outlasted the French and they could outlast the Americans too. Rebuffed, Johnson ordered Rolling Thunder to recommence on May 18.

Chinese military and economic assistance, as well as political support proved to be instrumental in Hanoi being able to weather the American aerial onslaught.

At about the same time, General Westmoreland's concern over the deteriorating situation on the battlefield in South Vietnam and the perceived inability of the South Vietnamese army to stem a major communist offensive brought the issue of American ground troops and their role to the forefront, an issue that would have a direct and powerful bearing on determining the future course of the air campaign in the north. Both Admiral Sharp and General McConnell, the Air Force Chief of Staff, were arguing by June that any large-scale commitment of U.S. forces to the fight in South Vietnam should be accompanied by a vastly enhanced strategic air offensive to degrade North Vietnamese military capabilities. This would also buy time for the newly intervening American ground forces to hopefully turn the tide against the Viet Cong. Secretary McNamara, however, remained committed to the original strategy of applying gradual pressure through the continuation of the interdiction effort amid fears that a new, expanded bombing campaign would draw in the Soviet Union and China and/or harden Hanoi's stance toward negotiations. On July 27 Johnson endorsed McNamara's position and in doing so "relegated the air war against North Vietnam to a role secondary to the ground war in the South."[26]

Admiral Sharp later considered this a turning point in the war and an opportunity missed, later writing: "Our Rolling Thunder bombing program against North Vietnam got off to a painfully slow start and inched along in the most gradual increase in intensity. At the same time we decided to employ additional ground forces in South Vietnam and use them in active combat operations against the enemy. Despite [CIA Director] John McCone's perceptive waring vis-à-vis the implications of deploying those ground forces without making full use of our air power against the north, Secretary McNamara chose to do exactly that, i.e., to downgrade the U.S. air effort in North Vietnam and to concentrate on air and ground action in the south. This fateful decision contributed to our ultimate loss of South Vietnam as much as any other single action we took during our involvement. And underlying it all was an almost frantic diplomatic activity directed at getting negotiations started. Hanoi would analyze such activity as an indication that we were lacking in the will to fight."[27]

The first three months of Operation Rolling Thunder were telling for a number of reasons, because the limited and tightly controlled bombing campaign was the worst of both worlds: too weak a political tool to pressure Hanoi to the negotiating table and too costly an operational strategy for degrading North Vietnamese military capabilities to support the Viet Cong. Try as they might, over the course of the next three years neither U.S. military commanders nor those in the Johnson White House were able to find a way to reconcile these two conflicting realities.

Earlier on the bombing campaign highlighted the problematic challenge of fighting a limited war where political objectives and concerns often conflicted with operational effectiveness and sound military strategy. Nonetheless, bombing the North appeared on the surface a useful and low-cost way to advance multiple U.S. political and military objectives. It could signal American resolve and boost morale in Saigon. It could punish Hanoi for its continuing support to the Viet Cong and it could restrict the flow of men and supplies southward. All this while avoiding any large-scale—and unavoidable long-term—commitment of U.S. ground forces to a land war in Southeast Asia. In Rolling Thunder, Washington thought it had the answer.

In what would become a continuing theme throughout American involvement in Vietnam, U.S. leaders and their advisers repeatedly misread or misunderstood the

Laotian Air Operations

While the conflict playing out in Vietnam took center stage and occupied much of the world's attention in the 1960s, another notable civil war that pitted a Western-supported government against a building communist insurgency was entering its second decade in neighboring Laos. Although the ground war between the Royal Laotian forces and the Pathet Lao communist insurgents ebbed and flowed with neither side gaining the upper hand throughout the 1960s, the country soon became a major—and secret—theater of air operations for the United States. During the course of Rolling Thunder three accompanying and specialized air campaigns were conducted by the Americans in the skies over Laos.

Operation Barrel Roll. This operation actually pre-dated Rolling Thunder and grew out of a plea by the Laotian government for assistance in slowing the flow of supply to the Pathet Lao from North Vietnam. In December 1964, President Johnson secretly authorized limited American air strikes in the northeast border area of Laos. The Air Force and Navy, operating from bases in Thailand, South Vietnam, and the Gulf of Tonkin, employed a wide variety of strike aircraft, including B-52 bombers, to attack enemy supply depots, bridges, and transportation routes, as well as to seek out and destroy truck convoys during armed recce missions. Although the bombing had only marginal military impact on the Laotian civil war, it provided a strong psychological boost to the Royal Lao government. Barrel Roll ended in February 1973 when the United States completed its withdrawal from Vietnam.

Operation Steel Tiger. By the end of 1964 the Laotian panhandle, which contained the Ho Chi Minh Trail and other North Vietnamese infiltration routes, had become part of a major conduit into South Vietnam. To counter this flow of men and supply through the Laotian panhandle Johnson authorized Steel Tiger as an interdiction effort in April 1965. By mid-1965 the Americans were flying 1,000 sorties per month and by 1967 that number had increased to more than 3,000, over half of which were large B-52 strikes. Air Force C-130 gunships were also extensively used. The difficult terrain, North Vietnamese concealment techniques, and thick jungle canopy, however, often limited the effectiveness of the bombing. Although credited with destroying large quantities of supplies and forcing Hanoi to commit large numbers of personnel to keeping the Ho Chi Minh Trail functioning, Steel Tiger operations only had a marginal impact on the North's ability to prosecute the war in the South.

Operation Tiger Hound. A subsidiary operation to Steel Tiger that came into being in December 1965, this operation covered the far southern Laotian panhandle adjacent to the five northwestern provinces of South Vietnam as part of General Westmoreland's extended battlefield. Unlike Barrel Roll and Steel Tiger, air operations and interdiction efforts here fell under control of MACV. In 1968, Steel Tiger and Tiger Hound operations were consolidated into a single new effort, Operation Commando Hunt, to cover the entire Ho Chi Minh Trail.

North Vietnamese. First, what was viewed by those in Washington as a war of aggression and a land grab by the North was to those in the North the final chapter in the nationalist struggle for Vietnamese independence. Ho Chi Minh's alignment with the communist bloc was more of a means to achieve his nationalist goals, but the zero-sum nature of the Cold War and American ideological resoluteness excluded this as a central motivating factor in the conflict. Moreover, the idea of "losing to the communists" in a region where the United States had steadily argued for Western security, where America's reputation was at stake, painted the Johnson administration into a corner from which it could not easily extract itself. Second, the United States vastly underestimated the North's resolve and overestimated the psychological impact of bombing. Even in the face of strong evidence from World War II questioning the ability of bombing to break the will of the enemy, American hubris belied the willingness of the North Vietnamese leadership to accept a high degree of short-term punishment in pursuit of their long-term goals. Whether any U.S. bombing effort in 1965 would have pushed Hanoi to the breaking point still remains a point of contention, but certainly the limited air campaign instituted in March proved woefully inadequate.

Limited war also meant limited operational success. Even when missions were deemed successful, the results were often short lived. Bridges were quickly repaired, road craters filled, and alternative routes and supply methods devised. Increasingly all military activity south of the 20th parallel was done under the cover of night. The North Vietnamese also quickly learned to utilize the restricted and prohibited zones around Hanoi and Haiphong to store critical supplies and equipment or provide a safe haven from which their MiG fighters would operate without fear of retribution. Limited warfare, however, did not mean limited risks for Air Force and Navy pilots and many a hard—and often costly— lesson was learned in those early days of the air campaign. "Never go dueling with a flak site" became the mantra of many a squadron after suffering heavy losses, because planes were making multiple passes in their effort to silence air defenses. Mandated attack profiles and ingress routes against targets located near populated areas often placed pilots in highly vulnerable situations with little choice but to press forward through the worst of enemy defensive fire. Likewise, the predictability of American routines, tactics, and timing of air strikes made it easier for the North Vietnamese to be ready and able to counter the attacks. As with all previous American wars there was a steep learning curve in the early months of 1965 and just like their predecessors in past conflicts the pilots flying Rolling Thunder missions would adapt to this new type of warfare, learning from their mistakes, and doing the best they could in fighting the war they had.

4. A BUILDING WHIRLWIND

On May 18, 1965 Operation Rolling Thunder resumed after a brief five-day pause. As critics had predicted, the halt coming as it did after only ten weeks of limited and restricted bombing did nothing to change Hanoi's stance. It reflected more of a hope rather than a carefully scripted strategic calculation by the Johnson administration, as both the United States and North Vietnam were still at this stage feeling the other out and assessing the opponent's weaknesses and vulnerabilities. The respite did, however, offer time for American pilots to reflect and gather themselves after the initial adrenaline rush of going into combat for the first time had worn off. It also allowed them to steel themselves for what was now becoming a long-term and dangerous mission. The reality was setting in that the bombing campaign would not be the cakewalk many had expected.

Moreover, the continuing failure of the Saigon government to turn the tide of battle against the Viet Cong—even with ever-increasing U.S. assistance—would force President Johnson's hand by mid-year. Critically the American drift into a ground war in South Vietnam would ultimately result in a de facto restructuring of the air campaign's goals. Although the operational requirements for Rolling Thunder would remain largely intact, the center of gravity for the war would move southward to the South Vietnamese battlefield. It was here now that American troops and air power would break the back of the insurgency and force Hanoi to the negotiating table and not in the skies over North Vietnam. Or so Washington hoped.

A-4E Skyhawk of VA-72 attacks a train and rail cars north of Thanh Hoa, October 1965. (Photo Emil Buehler Library, National Naval Aviation Museum)

Navy F-8 Crusader streaks across the skies over North Vietnam.

The Bombing Rolls Northward

Aircraft from the USS *Coral Sea*, USS *Oriskany*, and USS *Bon Homme Richard* were back at it with the commencement of Rolling Thunder 15. On May 18, the Navy launched strikes in the central panhandle against the Hoan Lao barracks, the Chanh Hoi communication center, and the Phu Qui POL (petroleum, oil and lubricants) storage facility with good results. Two days later an 86-plane naval strike force of A-1s, A-4s, and F-8s inflicted heavy damage on the Phuc Lao naval base near Vinh. Clearing weather on May 22 also permitted the Air Force to conduct the first air attack north of the 20th parallel against the Quang Soui barracks, located about 35 miles north of Thanh Hoa. Forty F-105s armed with 750-pound bombs damaged or destroyed about one-third of the compound buildings in the attack.[1] On the same day, as part of a stepped-up propaganda effort, the Air Force dropped 500,000 leaflets over Ninh Binh urging the North Vietnamese people to stop supporting leaders who were waging war against their Vietnamese brethren in the south. This complemented similar ongoing leafleting operations by the by the VNAF in the southern panhandle.

From the end of May to the end of July the bombing campaign steadily moved northward, although "with the rapidity of a tortoise," according to Admiral Sharp.[2] The ammunition storage facility at Hoai An was hit repeatedly over several days in late May and again in early June by F-105s and by Air Force F-4 Phantoms of the 45th TFS based at Ubon, Thailand, in a strike role for the first time.[3] Staging areas, army barracks, and logistics facilities to

Above: Thorn in the side of the American attackers— the Thanh Hoa bridge, also known as the "Dragon's Jaw," repeatedly survived multiple Air Force and Navy attempts to destroy it during Rolling Thunder. (U.S. Navy photo)

Right: EB-66 electronic countermeasures aircraft leads an F-105 strike formation on a bombing mission, 1965. (Photo National Museum of the U.S. Air Force)

the west and northwest of Hanoi above the 20th parallel were struck for the first time by the Air Force in late June. Notable targets included the Son La military compound and the base at Dien Bien Phu near the Laotian border, which were considered hubs for infiltrating men and equipment into northern Laos in support of the communist Pathet Lao forces. A strike by 28 F-105s and F-4s on July 2 extensively damaged the barracks area and the Dien Bien Phu airfield; a follow up attack on the 8th resulted in some additional cratering of the runway. Other large strikes were mounted at the ammunition storage facilities in the Yen Bai and Yen Son areas some 100 miles northwest of Hanoi. On July 28 several F-105s from the 12th TFS dropped enormous M118 3,000-pound bombs on Thanh Hoa bridge for the first time, but once again the bridge escaped major damage.[4]

For its part the Navy continued to concentrate its efforts on targets around Vinh and in the Thanh Hoa area, while also flying increased armed recce missions as part of stepped-up interdiction efforts. During one such armed recce mission on June 25 northwest of Thanh Hoa, Commander Peter Mongilardi's A-4 Skyhawk was struck by 37-mm anti-aircraft fire, killing the newly appointed carrier air wing commander of CVW-15. He was the first carrier air wing commander (or CAG) lost, but unfortunately would not be the last. Another dark milestone took place on July 18 when the first A-6 Intruder flying off the USS *Independence* was lost during an attack on the Ham Rong port facilities on the Nam Ma River. A premature detonation of the plane's Mk-82 bomb load—a recurring problem in 1965—fatally crippled the Intruder, forcing Commander Jeremiah Denton and his weapons officer Lieutenant (j.g.) Michael Tschudy to eject. Both became prisoners of war at the Hanoi Hilton. Upon his release in 1973 Denton would later rise to the rank of Rear Admiral and become a U.S. Senator from Alabama in 1980.

Supplementing the Air Force and Navy strikes, VNAF Skyraider pilots continued to hammer enemy positions and lines of communication in the southern panhandle with 500-pound Mk-82 bombs, as well as rocket and 20-mm cannon fire. The combined American and South Vietnamese effort resulted in 6,861 sorties by July 22, more than a tenfold increase since the beginning of the air campaign. More than 10,000 tons of bombs had been dropped, along with nearly 4,000 rockets expended.[5] The Air Force with its larger-capacity F-105s was responsible for dropping 55 percent of the ordnance, the Navy 32 percent, and the VNAF 13 percent.[6] This was not, however, without cost. Since the resumption of the bombing campaign in mid-May, two dozen additional American aircraft had been lost, including the first A-6 Intruder and F-4 Phantom losses, as well as the first U.S. plane downed by a surface-to-air missile. Sixteen more pilots and crew had also been killed.[7] This brought the total to 63 aircraft lost in combat and operational accidents since the start of Rolling Thunder.[8]

Even as the bombing move northward that summer too many key targets remained off limits, especially in the Hanoi and Haiphong areas, much to the frustration of military commanders. As Chief of Staff of the Air Force General McConnell critically noted, less than one-quarter of the 94 primary targets on the Joint Chiefs list (most north of the 20th parallel) had been attacked and existing targeting procedures and bombing restrictions were making it nearly impossible to destroy the will and capability of Hanoi.[9] A more aggressive air campaign was needed. Faced with the option of drastically escalating the air war in the North, McNamara after visiting Saigon in July recommended that the President stay the course and instead focus attention on reversing the tide on the battlefield in South Vietnam with an influx of American combat troops. After much internal debate

F-105D loaded up with 750-pounds bombs, Takhli Royal Thai Air Base. (Photo National Museum of the U.S. Air Force)

Fuel-guzzling Air Force F-4 Phantoms from their bases in Thailand required constant aerial tanker support for the combat operations over the far northwest and around Hanoi. (Photo National Museum of the U.S. Air Force)

within the administration, on July 28, 1965 Johnson publicly announced his intention to increase the size of U.S. forces in Vietnam by 50,000 men, bring the total to 125,000 and to double the size of monthly draft call-ups in the United States. The President also noted that "additional forces will be needed later," McNamara and Westmoreland privately telling the President that another 100,000 men could be needed in early 1966.[10]

Although overlooked at time, given fast-moving events and a string of policy decisions, Johnson's de facto commitment in the summer of 1965 to fighting a ground war in South Vietnam signaled a significant turning point. The use of air power in the North as a tool of coercive diplomacy was being replaced by a strategy that sought military victory on the battlefield in the South. As McNamara put it bluntly, "I do not want one plane dropping bombs on North Vietnam if it can be used advantageously for air operations in South Vietnam."[11] Defeating the Viet Cong, interdicting supply lines, and demonstrating the futility of North Vietnamese support for the insurgency would now become the critical leverage points for the United States. Thus, without realizing it at the time, the coercive elements of the air campaign in the North would become subjugated to the demands of the new military strategy in the South. This would turn the political objectives of Rolling Thunder into military ones, but without loosening the restrictions necessary to wage an effective strategic bombing campaign that this would entail.

Hanoi Girds its Defenses

Even as the United States was struggling to align the political and military objectives of the bombing campaign, Hanoi had one simple goal: strengthen its air defenses and in doing so make the Americans pay a rising price for their attacks. Thanks to the highly restricted and gradual nature of the air campaign the North Vietnamese were able to make major strides in building up their defenses north of the 20th parallel during the first half of 1965. By the time American warplanes began to attack targets in the Hanoi and Haiphong areas in earnest (although still outside the respective cities' restricted zones), the enemy was well-prepared and waiting to meet them. Herein lies the crux of the criticism of Rolling Thunder that had the United States undertaken an aggressive and largely unrestricted bombing campaign from the outset when the North Vietnamese were less prepared, the likelihood of success would have been far greater and the war would have been shortened. One will never know if air power alone could have been decisive in driving Ho Chi Minh to the negotiating table in 1965, but certainly the pilots flying the missions would have faced less capable and weaker air defenses and thus able to inflict more damage in a shorter period of time.

The most deadly and pervasive component of the north's air defenses was without a doubt its anti-aircraft weaponry. This would come to include everything from

North Vietnamese AAA gunners. It was their wall of lead that accounted for around two-thirds of American air casualties in the air campaign.

smaller-caliber crew-served guns to radar-guided heavy anti-aircraft artillery systems. As American pilots were to learn, the use of "sector firing" made these weapons extremely deadly. For rather than attempting to track and lead individual planes, North Vietnamese gunners simply filled the air with flak from 3,000 to 20,000 feet over the likely approach, forcing the attacking planes to fly through a steady stream of anti-aircraft fire. Thus, the basic laws of probability made low-level bombing, especially against fixed targets like bridges, an extremely hazardous business for American aviators. The first four months of Rolling Thunder drove this point home, with the loss of 54 aircraft—25 Navy, 22 Air Force, and seven VNAF—to enemy anti-aircraft fire and another 161 damaged.[12]

Prior to the start of the bombing campaign U.S. intelligence estimated that the North Vietnamese possessed 943 anti-aircraft guns of various calibers ranging from light

North Vietnamese machine-gunners, armed with a World War II-vintage German MG34, in an anti-aircraft role.

North Vietnamese AA gunners seen here with a 12.7-mm. "Sometimes it seemed like everyone down there was shooting at you," recalled one pilot.

North Vietnamese SA-2 surface-to-air missiles claimed their first victory on July 24, 1965 when they downed an Air Force F-4 northeast of Hanoi. The 35-foot long "flying telephone poles" had an effective range of 25 to 31 miles and could reach altitudes of nearly 60,000 feet. (Photo National Museum of the U.S. Air Force)

14.5-mm and 37-mm guns to heavier 57-mm, and 85-mm guns.[13] The latter group of heavier weapons accounted for about two-thirds of their anti-aircraft inventory. Hanoi also had at its disposal a handful of highly mobile ZSU-57-2 weapons. The number of anti-aircraft weapons would grow threefold by late summer and by the end of 1966 it was estimated that the North Vietnamese were able to field between 6,000 and 7,000 guns greater than 20-mm.[14] Thus, for this element of Hanoi's air defense strategy it was all about quantity: the more the better. The American effort to knock out the high-profile Thanh Hoa bridge is illustrative. Shortly after the bridge-busting campaign began in early April 1965, the North Vietnamese greatly reinforced their anti-aircraft defenses around the bridge, knowing that the Americans would continue to strike it until they knocked it out. And they were right. Air Force and Navy pilots flew repeated costly missions against the bridge and its defenses, which by April 29 consisted of 19 occupied anti-aircraft sites containing 110 light and medium weapons, according to photo reconnaissance.[15]

Although the potential danger posed by the relatively small North Vietnamese air force—known officially as the Vietnamese People's Air Force (VPAF)—was a deep concern for American planners, the VPAF's 66 MiG-15 and MiG-17 fighters avoided engaging U.S. aircraft in the early month of Rolling Thunder.[16] All this changed in early

April 1965 when MiG-17 fighters conducted hit and run attacks against American planes striking the Dong Phuong Thuong and Thanh Hoa bridges, downing two F-105s and damaging one F-8. These were the first air-to-air losses of the war for the Americans. The unexpected appearance of the MiGs and the ill-preparedness of the U.S. strike force was a wake-up call, because everyone knew it was coming and American fighter pilots had long been spoiling for a fight. Yet, they were caught flatfooted and it would be several months before they would get a chance to redeem themselves.

Many pilots and commanders blamed obstructive aerial rules of engagement for the losses, which catalogued when, where and how enemy aircraft could be engaged and pursued and prohibited attacks on the main MiG airfields in the Hanoi area. Less discussed, at least initially, was the poor showing of U.S. fighter tactics that had been allowed to atrophy in the modern era of long-range missile aerial engagements. Old time, close-in dogfighting was passé, or so was the assumption. In point of fact, the F-8C Crusader was only equipped with four Sidewinder air-to-air missiles and was not equipped with any guns (although later F-8 models sported multiple 20-mm cannons). In time, American fighter pilots would relearn the vital aerial combat lessons of World War II and Korea and the Navy would institutionalize this in training by creating the Naval Fighter Weapons School or Top Gun in 1969, which would pay dividends in the final years of the war. In the meantime, it was on-the-job training for each newly arriving air wing and fighter squadron.

The first MiG kills occurred on June 17, 1965 when two F-4 Phantoms of VF-21 off the USS *Midway* engaged a flight of four MiG-17s north of Thanh Hoa. Using Sparrow air-to-air missiles the Phantom pilots downed two of the MiGs. Three days later, a flight of A-1 Skyraiders also off the *Midway* shot down another MiG-17 in one of the more unusual dogfights of the war. The Air Force would have to wait a bit longer to get its first victories. On July 10 a flight of four F-4s flying cover for an F-105 strike, but mimicking a similar strike profile as the Thunderchiefs, engaged two attacking MiG-17s over the Yen Bai area 35 miles northwest of Hanoi. The attacking MiGs fired and missed with their guns before quickly breaking off. Two F-4s of the 45th TFS out of Ubon were able to fire off eight Sidewinder missiles. Two found their mark, blasting two MiGs from the sky.[17] For the remainder of the year, VPAF fighter pilots would periodically stage hit and run attacks against U.S. strike formations, but these limited efforts were not enough to disrupt the bombing. However, a new form of air threat was looming that would soon occupy the Americans' attention.

The construction of the first North Vietnamese SA-2 surface-to-air missile (SAM) site, 17 miles southeast of Hanoi, was first observed by U.S. reconnaissance aircraft flying a Blue Tree photographic mission on April 5, 1965. Washington, however, prohibited attacks against all SAM sites under construction for fear of killing Soviet or Chinese workers. Moreover, at least one senior U.S. defense official personally thought it doubtful that the North Vietnamese would ever use them; the missiles were merely "a political ploy by the Russians to appease Hanoi" and therefore he believed that they posed little danger to Rolling Thunder missions.[18] Thus, Hanoi's building of its missile defense network went unchallenged by the Americans and by late July a total of 23 SA-2 sites had been identified by U.S. intelligence.[19] At the end of the year this number would rise to at least 64, although only about one-third of the sites were ever active at any one time as the North Vietnamese constantly shuffled missile launchers, men, and equipment around to keep the American guessing. Roughly 60 percent of the SAM sites were located within 35 miles of Hanoi and another 20 percent could be found around Haiphong.

Dogfight: Spads vs. MiGs

On the afternoon of June 20, 1965 one of the truly unique dogfights of the Vietnam War took place in the skies over North Vietnam some 50 miles northwest of Thanh Hoa when a flight of four A-1 Skyraider (fondly known as "Spads") from the USS *Midway* were jumped by two North Vietnamese MiG-17 fighters. Flying at 10,000 feet under a layer of high clouds, the VA-25 flight led by Lieutenant Commander Ed Greathouse and his wingman, Lieutenant (j.g.) Jim Lynne were in front closely followed by a second two-plane section flown by Lieutenant Clint Johnson and Lieutenant (j.g.) Charlie Hartman. The VA-25 pilots had been assigned to fly a rescue patrol mission in response to a downed Air Force pilot in the Dien Bein Phu area. The mission this day would become like no other.

As the four Spads flew inland a U.S. destroyer patrolling offshore picked up incoming enemy aircraft heading in their direction. "Canasta [VA-25's call-sign], there are bandits in the air." And a few seconds later, "They are on your six o'clock at four miles. There are two of them." Hartman was the first to see the MiGs to the left of the American formation, about a mile off and flying at 10,500 feet. "I don't mind telling you that my heart was really pumping. I was stunned. You don't see enemy fighters every day in your life," he later recalled. The fast-approaching MiGs blew past the American planes without spotting them, possibly because the A-1s were just below the overcast. Realizing their mistake or having enemy ground radar vector them, the MiG-17s quickly reversed course back toward Greathouse and his men. All six aircraft were now closing, head on at 600 knots.

Outgunned and out-powered, the Spads executed split-S maneuvers and dove for the trees. Soon the MiGs were pursuing the Spads along a river valley flanked by steep ridgelines rising up to 2,000 feet. Following the river and trying to stay below 500 feet and occasionally dipping to 50 feet above the treetops, the American pilots sought to use the Spad's "down low and slow" capability and dangerous terrain to their advantage against the high-performance enemy jets. Just as one of the MiG's got a bead on Hartman, Greathouse fortuitously ordered all planes to release their 300-gallon external fuel tanks to increase their maneuverability. Hartman's plane seemingly leapt straight up in the air just as the tracers from the MiG ripped through the sky where his plane had just been. The enemy fighter then executed a sharp turn and made toward the north, possibly because he was running low on fuel.

Meanwhile, the second MiG-17 was relentlessly pursuing Greathouse and Lynne as they flew flat out at 225 knots while dipping and jinking their planes in an effort to shake the MiG. Soon a swirling fight ensued, involving four or five full-circle turns as each side tried to get into a firing position. "It was like being in a mixmaster," remembers Hartman. As the MiG pulled into position to line up a shot on Greathouse and Lynne, Johnson and Hartman found themselves head-on facing the MiG. They opened up immediately with their 20-mm cannons. It was later determined that 140 rounds were unleashed. The MiG's canopy shattered under the hail of bullets and the plane began trailing fire and smoke as it flew past Johnson and Hartman before slamming into a ridge and erupting into a fireball.

The dogfight lasted only about three minutes. All four pilots and their aircraft returned safely to the USS *Midway*, landing after dark. Johnson and Hartman were awarded Silver Stars and each credited with one-half a MiG kill. Greathouse and Lynne received the Distinguished Flying Cross for their actions.

(Adapted from R. Burgess and R. Rausa, *US Navy A-1 Skyraider Units of the Vietnam War*, pp. 20-22.)

The Soviet-made SA-2 surface-to-air missiles came into service in the U.S.S.R. in the late 1950s and were roughly 35 feet long—giving them the moniker of "flying telephone poles" by American pilots. With an effective range of 25 to 31 miles and a ceiling of nearly 60,000 feet they posed a new level of threat.[20] Powered by a two-stage solid rocket fuel system, each missile carried a 350-pound warhead of high explosive that could be fused either by contact, proximity or command detonation. A warhead detonating within 200 feet of an aircraft was lethal.

A typical North Vietnamese SAM site consisted of four to six launchers laid out in a star-shaped pattern with a central command van and other support equipment at the

Classic star-shape surface-to-air missile site: SA-2 missile launchers positioned on the perimeter, communication and command vans (center), and Fong Son radar (upper right). Roughly 60 percent of all SAM sites were located within 35 miles of Hanoi and another 20 percent could be found around Haiphong. (Photo National Museum of the U.S. Air Force)

center along with a Fong Song guidance radar located nearby. [21] The SAM batteries were highly mobile and could reportedly be stood up or broken down in as little as four hours. Separate anti-aircraft emplacements were frequently co-located near all missile sites to provide extra defense and discourage low-level attacks; SA-2s were ineffective below 3,000 feet. Soviet doctrine, adapted by the North Vietnamese, called for the missiles to be fired in pairs a few seconds apart with the hope that the first missile would occupy the pilot's full attention allowing the trailing second missile to home in on the target as it sought to evade the first missile. [22]

Evading SAM missiles tested not only a pilot's skill, but also his nerves, especially in those early days as the threat was evolving and U.S. countermeasures had yet to be fully developed. "The key to beating SAMs was early sighting [and] pilots learned to avoid hugging the cloud decks since the missiles could pop up undetected through the undercast. In reasonable weather, the telltale dust cloud, which indicated a launch, was the best visual cue. Timing was crucial in evading [because] if a pilot broke into his evasion too early, the missile had time to correct and continue tracking. If he waited a couple of seconds too long, he couldn't compensate in time. But the missile [was] subject to the same physical laws governing manned aircraft. Consequently, smart aviators always turned in two planes simultaneously to compound the difficulty of the missile's tracking. A barrel roll turn, keeping the SAM 30 to 40 degrees off the nose, was optimum. [Nonetheless] surviving a SAM launch became an exercise in sweaty-palm patience and pulse-pounding judgement." [23]

On the July 24 an Air Force F-4 from the 47th TFS was shot down by a SAM while flying combat air patrol during a strike on the Lang Chi munition factory northeast of Hanoi. [24]

Vietnamese People's Air Force MiG-17 pilots in front of their aircraft, circa 1966. (Photo National Museum of the U.S. Air Force)

This would be the first American aircraft lost to North Vietnamese surface-to-air missiles, but it wouldn't be the last. The Navy would lose its first plane, an A-4 from VA-23 flying off the *Midway*, to an SA-2 missile during a night recce mission on August 11 northwest of Thanh Hoa.[25] Following both losses, the Americans quickly launched retaliatory missions to locate and destroy the offending missile sites. Both efforts were disastrous. The Air Force launched a series of attacks against two SAM sites west of Hanoi on 27 July. Using 750-pound bombs, napalm, and rockets, 48 F-105s pounded the two positions while facing intense anti-aircraft fire as they dove low to avoid volleys of missiles. When it was all over both SAM sites were heavily damaged, but at a very high cost: three Thunderchiefs had been shot down by anti-aircraft or small-arms fire over the target areas, while two more heavily damaged planes were nursed back to Thai space before going down. Three pilots were killed, one captured, and one was rescued. The Navy likewise fared no better during its SAM hunt on August 12–13. Over the course of these two days, pilots from the *Coral Sea* and *Midway* flew 76 sorties in a futile attempt to locate and destroy occupied SAM sites. The effort, however, would cost them five aircraft and two pilots.[26]

As would happen throughout the air campaign, U.S. operational commanders were forced to learn (and even re-learn) some hard lessons about Hanoi's air defenses. The Navy responded to the new threat by equipping their planes with SAM launch warning electronics to give their pilots time to take evasion action and by designating one or more flights of A-4 to fly "Iron Hands"—SAM suppression missions—in high-threat environments. On October 17, 1965 Skyhawk Iron Hands from the USS *Independence* got the first confirmed kill of the war when they destroyed an operational SAM site near Kep airfield.[27] The Air Force, for its part, responded initially by adding more specialized electronic countermeasures (ECM) aircraft, such as the EB-66, to provide advance warning of active SAM sites and relied on flak suppression F-105s to take out the offending site. Eventually, however, the 2nd Air Division acquired about a half dozen specially modified twin-seat F-100Fs. Based out of Korat, Thailand, and attached to the 6234th TFW, these F-100Fs "Wild Weasels" with their sophisticated electronics pods would precede the strike force to the target area and would be the last to leave. If a SAM site came on line, the Wild Weasels would roll in to attack with rockets and mark the position for trailing F-105s armed with bombs and cluster munitions. It was a steep learning curve, however,

North Vietnamese MiG-21 deploying braking chute upon landing. (Photo National Museum of the U.S. Air Force)

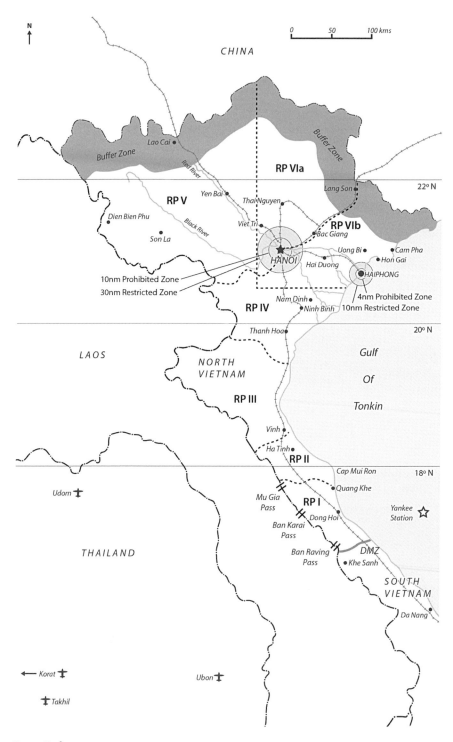

Route Packages.

with one of the first Wild Weasels being brought down by anti-aircraft fire near Kep on December 20. The Wild Weasels would get their payback two days later during a strike on the railroad yard at Yen Bai when they located and destroyed a SAM site targeting the strike force.[28]

Over time these measures, as well as evolving tactics and newly arriving technology would greatly diminish the missile threat. For instance, in 1965 one out of every 17 SAMs fired would shoot down a plane, but by 1966 twice that number was required and by the end of the war the overall ratio of missiles to losses had risen to 60 fired per kill.[29] While SAMs and even MiG fighters could be deadly, it was the high rate and volume of small-arms and anti-aircraft fire that would continue to inflict the most damage on attacking American planes throughout the course of Rolling Thunder.

Preparing for the Long Haul

Even as the bombing campaign was closing in on Hanoi and Haiphong it was becoming quite apparent to all that there would be no quick victory. Washington's focus by late 1965, moreover, was increasingly on winning the ground war in the South and supporting the American military buildup there. Air operations in the North, while still politically important, would likely play second fiddle to the new priorities. Accordingly, both the Air Force and Navy began making preparations for an extended air campaign into 1966 and possibly beyond. Even so, some senior Johnson administration officials held out hope that just a little more of the right kind of pressure would finally yield the results they desired. They were wrong.

The steady growth of Air Force personnel and aircraft deployed to South Vietnam and Thailand by mid-1965 and the increasing burden of the air campaign warranted a serious reassessment of the existing organization and policies. In July, Major General Moore established the first permanent tactical fighter wing in Thailand when the 6234th (Provisional) became the 6234th TFW. At the same time General McConnell placed Moore's 2nd Air Division directly under Pacific Air Force command for operational purposes. At General Westmoreland's behest, Moore would also now serve as MACV

F-100 Super Sabres at Da Nang, 1965. (Photo National Museum of the U.S. Air Force)

Takhli Royal Thai Air Base quickly became a major operational hub for F-105 squadrons starting with the deployment of the 6441st (Provincial) Tactical Fighter Wing in May 1965. (Author photo)

Deputy Commander for Air Operations in an attempt to harmonize Army, Air Force, and Navy efforts in South Vietnam.[30] The biggest change would be the shift from assigning units on a 120-day temporary duty status to a permanent one-year duty assignment. This change was long overdue. In June and July, for instance, all four F-105 squadrons in Thailand were rotated out to bring in a fresh crop of unseasoned pilots and a void in institutional memory. The change to a one-year deployment by the end of 1965 greatly reduced the churn of units, created a more effective operational environment, and allowed for a better mix of new and combat veteran aviators. The first F-105 squadron deployed for a one-year tour, the 333rd TFS, arrived at Takhil Royal Thai Air Force Base in early December.[31] Plans were also put in place to expand and streamline the support personnel and reconnaissance, communication, and electronic countermeasure units being sent to Thai air bases. Construction of new air bases in Thailand and South Vietnam to accommodate the increases became a top priority too.

The Navy for its part had an easier time ramping up for sustained air operations by simply redeploying more aircraft carriers to Southeast Asia. The two to three carriers on Yankee Station would rise to a normal complement of three to four by the end of the year with an additional ship positioned at Dixie Station (the Seventh Fleet staging area located

F-105Ds on the flight line at Takhil, Thailand, circa 1966. (Photo National Museum of the U.S. Air Force)

Air Force anti-SAM and flak suppression missions were conducted by the specially equipped F-105F "Wild Weasels," which began replacing the makeshift F-100Fs in May 1966. (Photo National Museum of the U.S. Air Force)

"Home of the Wolf Pack," the headquarters of the 8th TFW and its F-4 fighter squadrons at Ubon, Thailand. (Photo National Museum of the U.S. Air Force)

roughly 80 miles east of Cam Ranh Bay) to support combat operations in South Vietnam. This would provide Admiral Sharp with up to four air wings, totaling roughly 280 aircraft, to conduct Rolling Thunder missions. In time, however, this enormous commitment of men and equipment would severely strain naval resources and by mid-1967 of the Navy's 16 available carriers, 13 undertook at least one six-month Vietnam combat tour. Six ships—including the ageing World War II veteran carriers, USS *Hancock* and USS *Bon Homme Richard*—already served or were serving their third tour by this time.[32] Facing an increased demand for replacement pilots, the Navy also began shifting to a war footing, pushing new fleet pilots through the training pipeline as quickly as possible.

As the air threat environment grew more dangerous with the march northward and Hanoi's strengthening of its air defenses, air commanders saw the need to allocate specialized support aircraft and mission-specific aircraft to all large-scale, or "alpha," strike packages. Gone were the days of sending three or four dozen attack aircraft supported by only a couple of flak suppressors against a major target. By 1966, a typical Navy alpha strike would be composed of 12 attack aircraft rolling in on the target and supported by at least another 14 planes: four aircraft dedicated to SAM suppression, four conducting flak suppression, at least two fighters flying tactical combat air patrol with another two to four fighters farther out providing MiG cover, plus one or more ECM aircraft and one to two tankers operating offshore.[33] Flying out of more distant bases in Thailand, Air Force alpha strikes would often include even more supporting aircraft, including several KC-135 tankers plus their fighter escorts.

One of the more significant changes in late 1965 was to formalize and institutionalize the geographic division of North Vietnamese airspace between the Air Force and the Navy. Once put in place these seven administrative divisions, known as "route packages" or "route packs," would last until war's end. Starting at the southern panhandle, Route Pack I extended from the DMZ to about 20 miles north of Dong Hoi. Route Pack II then covered the area northward to just south of Vinh city.

B-52 heavy bombers on the flight line at Anderson Air Force Base in Guam. The bombers were used sparingly in Rolling Thunder, primarily in interdiction efforts in the far southern panhandle of North Vietnam and against the mountain passes into Laos. (Photo National Museum of the U.S. Air Force)

The Navy maintained a near constant presence of three to four aircraft carriers on Yankee Station in the Gulf of Tonkin throughout the air campaign, forcing some carriers such as the USS *Coral Sea* (pictured) and their squadrons into extended combat deployments. (Photo Naval History and Heritage Command)

Route Pack III went from Vinh to just south of Thanh Hoa. While Route Pack IV then covered the area from Thanh Hoa to Nam Dinh and south of Hanoi to the Laotian border. Route Pack V (the largest in area) extended from some 25 miles west of Hanoi all the way to the Laotian border. Route Pack VI, which covered Hanoi, was divided into two sub-packages approximately along the rail line running from Hanoi to Lang Son. Route Pack VI A extended west and north of this line, while Route Pack VI B extended east and south and included Haiphong.

Initially route package assignments were to be rotated between the Air Force and the Navy every two weeks along with a high degree of flexibility of diverting aircraft to the other's operational area if needed.[34] In short order, however, the Navy took primary control over flying Route Packs II, III, IV, and VI B, while the Air Force handled missions in Route Packs I (along with the VNAF), V, and VI A. Special permission would still be required under the rules of engagement for missions in the Hanoi and Haiphong prohibited and restricted zones and these would be assigned to either the Navy or Air Force on a case-by-case basis. The arrangement maximized the Navy's carrier operations given the largely coastal area of operations, but put the Air Force at a disadvantage of having to fly long distances from bases in Thailand over Laos and into the far northwest of Vietnam.

Toward on Uncertain Future

Even as the scope and nature of future American involvement in Vietnam was being hashed out at the highest levels of the U.S. government, air commanders continued to prosecute the air war in the North under the orders they had. Day after day in the final four months of 1965, pilots and air crews continued to strap themselves into the cockpit and fly the missions they were given. They didn't always like it. They often grumbled about McNamara's "limited war," the restrictive rules of engagement, and the number crunchers at the Pentagon, but they were professionals and they did their job. Although that job was becoming increasingly more dangerous as the campaign moved into the heavily defended northern part of the country.

While continuing to keep the pressure on logistics hubs at Thanh Hoa, Vinh, and Dong Hoi, as well as on lines of communication south of the 20th parallel, both the Air Force and the Navy stepped up activity north of the 21st parallel in advance of October monsoon season. From Nam Dinh and Hai Doung southeast of Hanoi to Thai Nguyen due north of the capital and to Yen Bai and Son La in the west, American warplanes unleashed their bombs and rockets on bridges, barracks, ammunition depots, key road junctions, and radar and communication sites throughout the remainder of the year. Likewise, dozens of aircraft flying armed recce missions both day and night sought out and attacked targets of opportunity, like trucks, trains and rolling stock, ferries, and watercraft. The heretofore, largely untouched northeast of the country began to be heavily targeted too, especially bridges along the Hanoi–Lang Son rail line that ran into China. On October 17 the Navy scored its first SAM kill when an A-6 Intruder and four A-4 Skyhawks flying an Iron Hand mission struck a newly discovered site near Kep airfield, northwest of Hanoi. The attackers pummeled the site with 500-pound and 1,000-pound bombs, leaving SA-2 missiles, transporters, and command and control vans in flames.[35] The Air Force also mounted several efforts to knock out the Dragon's Jaw bridge at Thanh Hoa; but with the same poor results the bridge still remained standing.

Navy ordnance men load an AIM-9 Sidewinder air-to-air missile on an F-8 Crusader. (Photo Emil Buehler Library, National Naval Aviation Museum)

As the strikes began to grow closer to Hanoi the air campaign showed some potential signs of success, but targeting restrictions, restrictive rules of engagement, sortie limits, and the deteriorating flying weather hindered the effort. Appeals by Admiral Sharp and General McConnell to widen and intensify the bombing of the North were rebuffed, as the White House and McNamara became increasingly consumed by the South Vietnamese counterinsurgency challenge. Yet the cost of the air campaign in terms of men and equipment was rising as the missions were now increasingly being flown into the teeth of the North Vietnamese air defenses.

A three-week period at the end of September into October 1965 starkly illustrated this reality. In preparation for a strike on the important Ninh Binh rail and highway bridge that carried traffic from Haiphong over the Song Day River, an Air Force RF-101C Voodoo was brought down by anti-aircraft fire while conducting a high-speed, low-level photo reconnaissance mission over the bridge on September 27. Three days later during the attack on the bridge an F-4C of the 47th TFS was shot down by heavy anti-aircraft weapons, along with an F-105D from the 334th TFS that was downed by an SA-2 missile. All three men were killed. Less than a week later, on October 5, Thai-based fighter squadrons suffered heavy losses during an attack on the Lang Mei bridge near Kep when two Thunderchiefs, one Phantom, and a Voodoo (conducting post-strike reconnaissance) were all downed by intense anti-aircraft fire. It was the Navy's turn on October 17. Three F-4Bs were lost during a 15-plane alpha strike by USS *Independence* aircraft against the

The entire range of Vietnam veteran aircraft carriers—from World War II to the nuclear age—berthed at Alameda, California in 1974. The USS *Coral Sea*, USS *Hancock*, USS *Oriskany*, and the USS *Enterprise* (left to right) spent a total of 3,187 total days on the line in Vietnam. (Photo Emil Buehler Library, National Naval Aviation Museum)

63

Thai Nguyen bridge, approximately 30 miles north of the capital. All three Phantoms were brought down by flak or small-arms fire, leaving two dead and four officers captured. Interestingly, two of the Phantoms were shot down by enemy flak not over the bridge itself, but on either the ingress or egress to the target. Flying anywhere north of the 21st parallel was becoming increasingly hazardous. These losses, combined with other combat losses, brought the total for this three-week period to 18 aircraft, nine dead, and eleven captured.[36]

By November White House approval was given to strike several major bridges along the Haiphong–Hanoi corridor that fell within both cities' restricted zone. Deteriorating weather conditions, however, forced the cancellation or postponement of hundreds of missions; the Air Force aborted 354 sorties alone from 28 October to 25 November.[37] Nonetheless, on November 7 the Air Force and the Navy mounted a concerted effort to take out the bridges. In the morning a 20-plane Navy alpha strike was flown against the bridge at Me Xa along the Haiphong–Hanoi corridor and in the face of heavy flak and SAM defenses. Later that afternoon, 15 Air Force F-4s hit the Phu Ly bridge south of the capital, while another 20 Air Force planes attacked two SAM sites near the Guoi Bo bridge that knocked out both positions. By the end of November at least 18 SAM sites had been struck by Navy and Air Force planes with varying degrees of success. On several occasions MiG-17 fighters made fleeting appearances—the first since early July—in an effort to disrupt photo reconnaissance missions or strikes, but they failed to engage the Americans.

Despite these successes, there was often a steep price to be paid as the USS *Oriskany* pilots of Carrier Air Wing 16 (CVW-16) found out when attacking the Hai Duong rail and highway bridge. The initial 20-plane strike on November 5 resulted in only minimal damage. One F-8E was lost to 57-mm anti-aircraft fire, while an A-4 Iron Hand mission scored a direct hit on an SA-2 missile launcher that resulted in a massive secondary explosion. Things got worse on the 17th during a maximum-effort alpha strike that included Crusaders carrying huge Mk-84 2,000-pound bombs. Over the course of 30 minutes two pilots were killed and four planes—three from CVW-16—were lost to 37-mm and 57-mm anti-aircraft fire; one of these was a Skyraider flying a rescue cover in an attempt to locate a downed pilot. Even more bitter news awaited the pilots on their return to the *Oriskany*: the bridge still remained operational.

In an effort to up the pressure on Hanoi to enter into negotiations, President Johnson authorized in early December a high-profile attack on the Uong Bi power plant located 12 miles northeast of Haiphong. The plant was considered one of the North's key industrial facilities and was estimated to provide about a quarter of the country's electricity. After several weather-related cancellations, 23 Air Force F-105s loaded with 750-pound, 1,000-pound, and enormous M118 3,000-pound bombs took off from bases in Thailand on December 15. The strike force was supported en route by several dozen Thunderchiefs, F-4 fighters, EB-66s, RF-101s, and KC-135 tankers.[38] The weather over the target was marginal at best and only seven F-105s, armed with two 3,000-pound bombs each, were able to make bombing runs. All the bombs fell wide of the mark and enemy anti-aircraft fire brought down one Thunderchief. The Navy had its turn on the night of 19th when six A-6 Intruders off the USS *Kitty Hawk* dropped Mk-84 2,000-pound bombs on the plant.[39] All missed. One of the Intruder and its two-man crew were lost to an SA-2 missile near Haiphong. A third strike was authorized for December 22 and this time about a hundred planes from the carriers *Enterprise*, *Kitty Hawk*, and *Ticonderoga* were dispatched to drop some 25 tons of bombs on the plant. Two A-4Cs from the *Enterprise* were shot down by anti-aircraft fire

The World War II-designed, A-1 Skyraider was flown by the Navy, Air Force, and VNAF. It became a workhorse in the early years of the war because of its versatility as a close air support and attack aircraft. Capable of carrying an 8,000-pound mixed load of ordnance, it could be armed with bombs ranging from 250 to 1,000 pounds, as well as cluster munitions, napalm, and 2.75- and 5-inch rockets. (Photo U.S. Navy)

Secretary of Defense Robert S. McNamara, 1961–68. (Photo Department of Defense)

General William C. Westmoreland, commander of Military Assistance Command, Vietnam (MACV), 1964–68; Chief of Staff of the Army, 1968–72. (Photo U.S. Army)

U.S. Navy personnel on ships operating off the coast of North Vietnam jokingly referred to themselves as members of the "Tonkin Gulf Yacht Club." (Photos Emil Buehler Library, National Naval Aviation Museum and Author)

Lieutenant Commander Jesse R. Emerson of VA-22 in his A-4C Skyhawk preparing to launch off the USS *Midway* during pre-deployment workups in February 1965. (Author photo)

First deployed in North Vietnam in June 1965, the twin seat A-6 Intruder attack aircraft provided the Navy with a reliable all-weather, day and night bombing capability that the Air Force sorely lacked. (Photo Emil Buehler Library, National Naval Aviation Museum)

White House meeting concerning Vietnam policy in July 1965: President Lyndon Johnson (center), Secretary Defense Robert McNamara (right), and National Security Council Advisor McGeorge Bundy (standing). (Photo LBJ Library)

The supersonic F-105D Thunderchief or "Thud" became the de facto workhorse of the Air Force's bombing campaign in North Vietnam, carrying 5,500-pound bomb payloads. Never designed for the mission, many Air Force pilots criticized the policy of conducting a strategic bombing campaign with a tactical fighter aircraft. (Photo National Museum of the U.S. Air Force)

The fast and highly maneuverable MiG-17 was the most widely used North Vietnamese fighter aircraft during Rolling Thunder. Employing hit and run tactics, MiG-17 pilots sought to disrupt American strike formations with their 37-mm and 23-mm cannons before fleeing to the safety of their bases. (Photo Air Force Inspection Agency)

The advanced, supersonic MiG-21 fighter, which was armed with cannons and air-to-air Atoll missiles, entered service in the VPAF in early 1966 and soon proved to be a capable counter to the American F-4 Phantom IIs. (File photo)

A Soviet S-60 57-mm piece, used very effectively by the North Vietnamese AAA gunners.

The F-4 Phantom II was not only one of the Navy's primary fighters, but saw extensively use as a tactical bomber and reconnaissance aircraft too. (Photo Emil Buehler Library, National Naval Aviation Museum)

Four A-1 "Sandys" lead a KC-130 and HH-53 "Jolly Green Giant" helicopter on an Air Force combat search and rescue mission into enemy territory. (Photo National Museum of the U.S. Air Force)

Air Force ground crew loading 20-mm rounds into an F-4 centerline gun pod (foreground); a row of yet-to-be-serviced gun pods is upper right. Initially armed with only air-to-air missiles, the F-4C was at a distinct disadvantage when engaging in close-in aerial combat with the cannon-equipped MiG-17s and MiG-21s. (Photo National Museum of the U.S. Air Force)

Colonel Robin Olds (second from right) celebrates completing his 100th mission with fellow Wolf Pack pilots of the 8th TFW at Ubon Royal Thai Air Base in September 1967. (Photo National Museum of the U.S. Air Force)

Armed with AGM-45 Shrike homing missiles, the two-seat F-105F or "Wild Weasel" provided flak and SAM suppression support to Air Force strike formations from Thai air bases. (Photo National Museum of the U.S. Air Force)

F-105D gun camera view of 20-mm cannon fire downing a MiG-17 on June 3, 1967 by Major Ralph Kuster of the 13th TFS out of Korat, Thailand. (Photo U.S. Air Force)

U.S. Air Force patch celebrating completing 100 F-105 combat missions.

The F-8 Crusader, known as the "Last of the Gunfighters," was one of the primary Navy fighters. Crusader pilots accounted for 18 of the Navy's MiG kills during Rolling Thunder. Its durability and versatility also made it an effective attack and reconnaissance aircraft during the air campaign. (Photo U.S. Navy)

The technologically advanced F-111 fighter was rushed into service in March 1968 and soon encountered multiple problems leading to the combat and operational loss of three aircraft within a month. They were withdrawn from combat after flying on 55 sorties. (Photo U.S. Air Force)

An A-4F Skyhawk with Mk-82 Snakeyes heads into combat, 1968.

A deadly fire aboard the USS *Forrestal* in the Gulf of Tonkin on July 29, 1967 left the aircraft carrier badly damaged, 134 men dead, and 62 injured.
(Photo U.S. Navy)

The burden of command, February 1968. President Lyndon Johnson and Secretary of Defense Robert McNamara deal with the consequences of the Tet Offensive, Johnson in divine supplication, McNamara not.
(Photo LBJ Library)

during their low-level bomb runs, but this time the plant was largely reduced to rubble.[40] The attack, however, failed to push Ho Chi Minh to the negotiating table.

With nearly all levels of the operational chain of command grumbling about the prosecution of the air campaign, both Sharp and McConnell advocated for more flexibility and a more focused strategic bombing effort. They correctly noted that multiple North Vietnamese vulnerabilities, such as supply shipments through Haiphong harbor, had yet to be exploited. Likewise, key airfields, industrial centers, and supply and storage depots in the immediate Hanoi and Haiphong environs had so far escaped the bombing. Just as Sharp and his staff were busy formulating plans to transform Rolling Thunder into a decisive tool to end the war in the next 12 to 18 months, President Johnson unexpectedly announced a 30-hour Christmas truce to begin on Christmas Eve.

The brief Christmas truce would soon turn into a prolonged 37-day bombing halt that would last into the end of January 1966 as Washington sought to build domestic U.S. support for the bombing campaign, as well as pursue public and behind-the-scene diplomatic efforts to end the conflict. In particular, Secretary McNamara held out hope that "a lengthy bombing pause would provide the Soviet Union [with whom the United States had been quietly in contact] with an opportunity to exert pressure on Hanoi to begin talks."[41] A highly pessimistic view of the state of the South Vietnamese counterinsurgency at the end of 1965, including Westmoreland's assessment that the United States might have to commit up to 600,000 troops by 1967 to achieve a military victory, appeared to tip the scales toward once again seeking a negotiated settlement. Not surprisingly, U.S. military commanders viewed the bombing halt as a serious strategic mistake, one that would allow Hanoi to repair bomb damage, reequip and resupply its forces, and further strengthen its air defenses. Thus, 1966 began with a high degree of anxiety and uncertainty as to the future of Rolling Thunder.

President Johnson and his advisers constantly struggled to find an effective strategy for curbing North Vietnamese aggression in the South without widening the war and risking a Cold War confrontation. (Photo LBJ Library)

5. FURY FROM ABOVE

As the bombing halt stretched into 1966, the Johnson administration embarked on a concerted diplomatic effort to jump-start negotiations with Hanoi. Although many of Johnson's advisers—as well as the President himself—were skeptical as to the chance of success, any peace overture was likely to shore up domestic political support for any future American escalation and play well to international public opinion. Accordingly, a high-profile effort was undertaken to show that Washington was open to talks with Hanoi. Over the course of January distinguished American diplomats and senior U.S. administration officials, including Vice-President Hubert Humphrey, visited 34 capitals around the globe touting the peace initiative.[1] As expected, Hanoi denounced the initiative as an American propaganda ploy: "deceitful and perfidious trickery."[2]

The timing for peace talks was simply not right as neither side was willing to make any meaningful concessions. The limited American bombing campaign had yet to inflict any critical damage or significantly hinder the North's ability to prosecute the war or support the Viet Cong. Likewise, the United States had yet to fully play the ground troop card, which it believed would shift the battlefield balance in favor of Saigon. Moreover, experience had taught Ho Chi Minh that time was on his side and so there was little cost to him in delaying peace talks.

The political gamesmanship and foot dragging in resuming the bombing campaign, however, rankled American military commanders. They saw it as a terrible

General John P. McConnell, Chief of Staff of the Air Force, 1965–69.

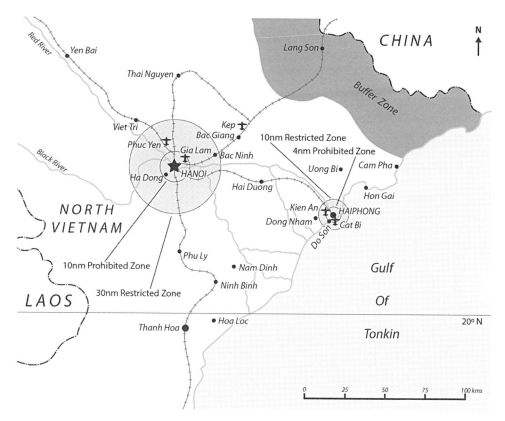

The North Vietnamese heartland.

strategic mistake. Admiral Sharp and General McConnell vigorously pushed for an immediate and aggressive resumption of the bombing. In a long message to the Joint Chiefs, Sharp laid out his case calling for a new reinvigorated campaign to cut all Hanoi's external supply sources, to destroy war resources already in the country and the North Vietnamese military infrastructure, and to continually harass, disrupt, and impede movement of men and matériel into South Vietnam.[3] According to Sharp, "this message outlined a course of action that in my judgment would have ended the war possibly by the end of 1966 and surely by the end of 1967."[4]

Back to Square One: The Bombing Resumes

On January 31, Operation Rolling Thunder resumed after a prolonged 37-day pause, but not at all as Sharp had envisioned. Missions were limited to only armed recces south of the 21st parallel, no strikes were approved for targets in the northeast or around Hanoi and Haiphong, and SAM suppression missions were confined to south of the 21st parallel.[5] Moreover, a limit of 300 sorties per day was imposed, a reduction of more than one-third of previous levels.[6] The monsoon weather further hampered even these limited efforts, with planes frequently being diverted to secondary targets or forced to jettison their bombs over the Gulf of Tonkin. To cope with these conditions, the Navy relied heavily on the all-weather A-6 Intruders, while the Air Force began to make use of B-66B pathfinder aircraft leading F-105s and F-4s on synchronous radar bombing runs at 15,000 feet, which soon accounted for almost 95 percent of all Air Force bombs dropped.[7] Even implementing these measures, the number of sorties failed to reach 3,000 in February. Thus, rather continuing to build on the momentum that had been achieved by the end of 1965 the air campaign was all but starting over.

As at the beginning of the campaign, strikes were heavily concentrated in Route Packs I, II, and III, especially against traffic along national Route 1 and coastal waterways. From Ha Tinh northward to Thanh Hoa armed recce missions sought out and attacked enemy vehicles, rail traffic, and watercraft moving supplies southward, as well as striking small bridges, ferries, and key road junctions. Special permission was granted to once again strike the key logistics hub at Dien Bien Phu and over the course of a week in mid-February F-105s rained 750-pound bombs down on the complex with mixed results. However, attempts to add additional targets in Route Pack V, especially along the Hanoi–Lao Cai rail line that brought in supplies from China, were rebuffed.

It was not just the Americans who were starting over. The North Vietnamese made good use of the prolonged bombing halt to rebuild or repair much of their damaged transportation infrastructure and to strengthen and resupply their air defenses. In early

The first Wild Weasel crews and their modified two-seat F-100F Super Sabres arrived at Korat Royal Thai Air Base in November 1965 and quickly found themselves caught up in a deadly cat and mouse game with North Vietnamese SAM batteries. (Photo National Museum of the U.S. Air Force)

1966 U.S. intelligence believed that the North had constructed nearly 14,000 anti-aircraft positions (about one-third occupied at any one time) and had some 20 to 25 SA-2 missile battalions rotating among some 100 identified sites.[8] Defenses along transportation routes and around key cities south of the 20th parallel now bristled with heavier-caliber anti-aircraft weapons, fire-guidance radars, and even SA-2 missile sites. The area between Thanh Hoa and Vinh was especially well outfitted. Thus, as American commanders had feared, the North Vietnamese were well prepared and ready when Rolling Thunder recommenced.

As if to drive home this point, a Navy A-4C Skyhawk flown by Commander Jack Snyder, the USS *Ticonderoga*'s CAG, was fatally crippled by an SA-2 missile explosion while conducting an armed recce 20 miles south of Thanh Hoa on February 9, the first lost to a SAM since December 22, 1965.[9] By mid-March, six more planes would be lost to SAMs, including an Air Force EB-66 ECM aircraft flying at 30,000 feet and operating just off the coast north of Vinh city.[10] In the first two month of resuming the bombing, a total of 29 American aircraft would be lost to North Vietnamese air defenses along with 24 pilots and crew.[11]

Despite these losses, the Americans were indeed making progress toward mitigating the SAM threat. The effectiveness of the Navy's A-4 Iron Hand missions was greatly enhanced with the introduction of the AGM-45 Shrike air-to-ground missile in March (although the Navy had been testing it in the North since late 1965). The ability of missile, equipped with a 150-pound warhead, to home in on not only the SAM's Fan Song guidance radar, but also other radar-guided heavy anti-aircraft weapons from 25 miles out increased the lethality of SAM and flak suppression missions. On April 18 an Air Force F-100F Wild Weasel launched its first Shrike against a suspected SAM site. In late May specially developed, two-seat F-105Fs, known as "Wild Weasel IIIs," joined the 388th TFW of the

North Vietnamese SA-2 site near Hanoi under attack by Air Force Wild Weasels that not only relied on AGM-45 Shrike homing missiles, but utilized bombs and 20-mm cannon fire to pulverize their targets. (Photo National Museum of the U.S. Air Force)

Seventh Air Force in Thailand (following the re-designation of the 2nd Air Division in April) and rising numbers of early warning and ECM aircraft in the fight against Hanoi's air defenses. By the middle of July Wild Weasel aircraft had expended over 100 Shrikes against SA-2 and heavy anti-aircraft gun radars.[12] Although the number of confirmed SAM kills was minimal—as North Vietnamese gunners learned to turn off their radars to disrupt the Shrike's homing ability—the continual threat of these missiles often acted as a deterrent to launching missiles in the first place.

Sharp's lobbying for a loosening of the White House reins on the bombing, including more operational flexibility, the addition of more targets north of the 21st parallel, and the ability to launch more attacks in the Hanoi and Haiphong restricted zones, eventually yielded results. While Sharp got some of what he wanted, McNamara's vacillation over the effectiveness of the bombing campaign so far, longstanding White House concerns over drawing the Soviets and Chinese into the war, and further political upheaval in Saigon that spring prevented the dramatic overhaul that Sharp had desired. Nonetheless, the White House agreed to expanded operations beginning April 1 by opening up most of Route Pack V, gave permission for a "controlled armed reconnaissance program" for Route Packs VI A and VI B, granted greater autonomy for operational requirements to field commanders, and agreed to a targeted monthly sortie rate of just over 5,000 that did not include supporting missions. Other restrictive rules, such as flying Iron Hand missions only against SAM sites in the armed recce areas and the prohibition against attacking VPAF airfields in the Hanoi–Haiphong area, however, remained in place.

Over the next several months Hanoi's transportation network in the northeast, as well as several important industrial and economic targets there came under renewed attack by American warplanes. In April alone naval aircraft from the USS *Ticonderoga* and USS *Kitty Hawk* put several major bridges out service, including the important Hai Duong bridge over the Thai Binh River between Haiphong and Hanoi, re-struck the partially repaired Uong Bi power station with A-6 Intruders during a nighttime operation that put it out of action again, and badly damaged the coal exporting facilities at the port of Cam Pha, only some 20 miles south of the Chinese border.[13] Meanwhile, Air Force planes were hitting major infrastructure targets to the north and west of Hanoi, including a highly successful 13-plane F-105 strike on the Thai Nguyen railyard northwest of the capital that inflicted major damage. Several main bridges along the rail line to the northeast, however, proved to be tougher nuts to crack. Over the course of two days in late April, the 388th TFW out of Korat, Thailand, would lose four F-105Ds to anti-aircraft fire and SA-2 missiles during attacks on the Phu Lang Thuong bridge; three pilots would be killed and one captured.[14] Knocking out the nearby Bac Giang rail bridge, some 25 miles northeast of Hanoi and close to Kep airfield, would be even more challenging. It would take five missions and behemoth M118 3,000-pound bombs to finally collapse several northern spans of the bridge on May 5. During this final mission, 1st Lieutenant Karl Richter found his F-105 caught in the blast wake from an M118 that had torn off his right stabilizer and badly holed the rear fuselage.[15] Fortunately, Richter was able to nurse his severely damaged Thunderchief back to Korat and both pilot and plane would live to fly another day. Other multiple strikes in May laid waste to the Yen Bai railyard and military storage to the northwest of Hanoi, although at the cost of several F-105s lost to withering enemy anti-aircraft fire. The missions in Route Pack V and VI A in April and May would cost the Air Force 23 Thunderchiefs.[16]

A Wild Weasel mission card detailing call signs, radio frequencies, and operation guidelines for "Scotch 1440" flight of May 14, 1967. (Photo National Museum of the U.S. Air Force)

Just as Rolling Thunder appeared to be getting back on track in the spring of 1966, General Westmoreland started advocating for a greater focus on interdiction efforts in the far southern panhandle and southern Laos. Westmoreland's view of what he called "the extended battlefield" found a receptive audience in McNamara and within the White House that was girding itself for an escalating ground war in the south: U.S. troop strength would rise to 385,000 by the end of the year.[17] The idea of placing planes and mission priorities under MACV control and diverting assets away from the air war in the northeast of the country was poorly received by the Air Force and the Navy. McNamara pressed forward anyway by declaring that "all commanders are to give first priority …

to fulfilling requirements ... against targets in the extended battlefield" and that other operations in North Vietnam "are not to be carried out unless they can be performed without penalty" to this priority area.[18]

As an indication of this priority the Joint Chiefs authorized the first B-52 bombing missions over North Vietnam. On April 11, 30 B-52 bombers dropped some 600 tons of bombs on the Mu Gia Pass adjacent to Route Pack I and astride the North Vietnamese–Laotian border in an effort to close the important supply route.[19] This attack was followed by another on the 17th, which heavily cratered the road through the pass and closed it temporarily. By June the Air Force was flying more than 3,800 interdiction sorties in Route Pack I and expending hundreds of tons of ordnance to cut the rail line between Vinh and the DMZ.[20] The Navy's Task Force 77 (TF-77) for its part was focusing its strikes against the logistic hub at Vinh and maintaining pressure on the Thanh Hoa–Vinh corridor with dozens of daily armed recce missions.

It was all for naught as the North Vietnamese found new and innovative ways to move men and matériel southward through an improvised network of jungle trails, dirt tracks, and small rivers that escaped the prying eyes of American pilots. Most critically, the expanded interdiction effort distracted from Admiral Sharp's central mission of escalating attacks on the critical northeast and punishing Hanoi. In contrast with earlier

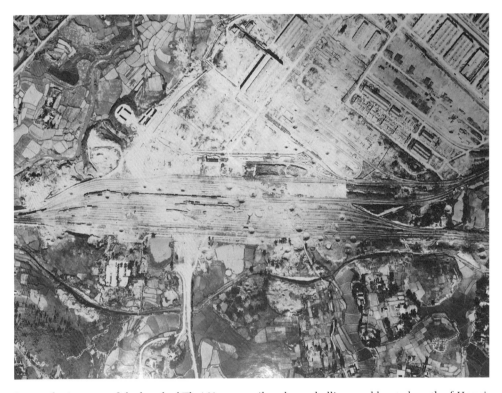

Post-strike imagery of the bombed Thai Nguyen railroad marshalling yard located north of Hanoi, which was hit repeatedly by the Air Force in an effort to sever transportation and communications links to the North Vietnamese capital. (Photo National Museum of the U.S. Air Force)

months, Air Force pilots flew a meager 98 sorties against key bridges, rail lines, railyards, and logistics sites in Route Packs V and VIA in June; just 2.6 percent of all their missions over the North. To further underscore the strategic importance of the northeast, a Joint Chiefs' assessment of Rolling Thunder's first year noted that while it had achieved "a degree of success within the parameters of imposed restrictions," only 57 percent of the 236 JCS targets had been attacked and highlighted that 70 of the remaining 102 untouched targets remained off limits, falling within the Hanoi–Haiphong restricted zones or within the buffer zone along the Chinese border.[21]

Upping the Ante

Competing military agendas and conflicting strategic objectives, as well as the Johnson administration's continued micromanagement of Rolling Thunder, combined to limit the bombing campaign's effectiveness throughout the first half of the year. In many respects, December 1965 was beginning to look like the high-water mark of the campaign, but then in June, Admiral Sharp was handed a gift. After years of debate, the White House gave its approval for an all-out effort to destroy North Vietnamese petroleum, oil, and lubricants (POL) infrastructure north of the 20th parallel, which accounted for nearly 90 percent of the country's supply.[22] Most telling the plan would include strikes against key POL storage facilities in Hanoi and Haiphong that were estimated to hold 46 percent of North Vietnamese POL stores.[23]

Weather delays and last minute postponements put off launching the joint Air Force–Navy strikes until June 29. The POL campaign opened with an attack on the main Haiphong storage site—with a capacity of 45,000 metric tonnes—by 28 aircraft from the USS *Constellation* and USS *Ranger*, including sixteen A-6 Intruders loaded with 250-pound and 1,000-pound bombs. Meanwhile, other naval aircraft also struck the smaller Don Son site immediately south of the port. To the west, a 63-plane Air Force strike force flying from its

POL storage site at Bac Giang northeast of Hanoi on fire after being struck by naval aircraft in the summer of 1966. (Photo Naval History and Heritage Command)

bases in Thailand focused its attention on a sprawling POL tank farm located only three and half miles from downtown Hanoi. Twenty-five F-105 Thunderchiefs delivered nearly 200 750-pound bombs on the facility, while other F-105s hammered anti-aircraft and SAM sites in the area, as two dozen F-4s patrolled the skies on the lookout for enemy MiG fighters. When it was all over the facility was ablaze and being rocked by secondary explosions; billowing smoke could be seen for miles. Post-strike analysis indicated that that over 90 percent of the target had been destroyed at the cost of one F-105D brought down by anti-aircraft fire. The Navy for its part was far less successful as many bombs fell wide of their intended targets, both Haiphong facilities suffering only minor damage. The North Vietnamese responded with public outrage and claimed that the attacks in the urban areas had caused extensive civilian casualties, but produced no proof.

Over the course of the next 12 days American planes returned daily to strike and restrike POL facilities in the face of heavy air defenses. One Air Force veteran of Korea (and now Vietnam) said, "It was worse than anything I've experienced."[24] Nguyen Khe, Viet Tri, and Phuc Yen lying north and northwest of the Hanoi were hit. Naval aircraft off the USS *Hancock* plastered the Bac Giang facility with 24 tons of bombs, hit Dong Nham northeast of Haiphong, and returned to attack the Haiphong and Don Son POL storage sites. Other smaller POL facilities in the Thanh Hoa area were struck, as were targets farther south at Phu Qui and Vinh city. By July 11 a total of 25 sites—accounting for 80–90 percent of the north's POL storage and facilities—had been bombed, resulting in the destruction of more than half of the facilities.[25] The deputy commander of the Seventh Air Force, Major General Gilbert Meyers, called the effort, "the most important strike of the war to date."[26]

Fuel storage tanks on the outskirts of Haiphong on fire in the aftermath of a U.S. Navy air strike during the summer of 1966. (Photo Naval History and Heritage Command)

The White House was elated with the results. So much so that President Johnson ordered McNamara in early July to give "strangulation of North Vietnam's POL system first priority."[27] Accordingly, the POL campaign saw an expansion of the armed recce area of operations to the entire country (with the exception of the buffer zone along the Chinese border and the restricted zones around Hanoi and Haiphong), an authorized raising of the sortie level to 10,000 per month, and added several important infrastructure targets. Soon American planes were striking the remaining fixed POL sites, bombing critical segments of Hanoi's rail and road network to disrupt the flow of replacement supplies from China, and began scouring the countryside for smaller dispersed POL storages areas.

The North Vietnamese, however, learned to adapt by intensifying their efforts to decentralize and disperse POL supplies and facilities to underground storage tanks and remote sites. Even 55-gallon drums were stockpiled by the thousands throughout villages and towns that remained off limits to American bombing. Soviet oil tankers too soon began to bypass Haiphong harbor and its heavily damaged storage facility to unload at Chinese ports for overland shipment into the North. Alternatively, they anchored offshore and then unloaded under the cover of darkness by a fleet of small barges. Although the barges were subject to attack under the rules of engagement, distinguishing them at night from the dozens of other civilian watercraft was difficult and during the day the barges moored alongside the "neutral tankers" for protection.

Anti-aircraft crews and SAM batteries were also ready and on high alert. Not only the Hanoi–Haiphong area, but also key cities along the central coast bristled with new weaponry. As one Navy Skyhawk pilot recalls, "There was a real drive to watch for threats, looking for SAM lift-offs, keeping your head on a swivel. Once you began your bombing run with the nose of plane pointing at the ground you were predictable anywhere from two to eight seconds and if the ground folks could see your roll in point, they might put up a barrage and there was a chance of getting hit. No rule prevented you from being hit in the run."[28]

And get hit they did. During two days in early August, for instance, ten American aircraft would be shot down over the North, costing the lives of three pilots with seven others captured.[29] Thus, because of diminishing returns—American planes had been able to locate and destroy only less than 10 percent of Hanoi's dispersed supplies—and the rising cost of both men and planes, Admiral Sharp decided to call an end to the strangulation effort on September 4.[30]

Even as the POL phase of the air campaign was drawing to a close the battle over the skies of North Vietnam was continuing to heat up as Admiral Sharp pushed—unsuccessfully—to maintain the momentum; the final four months of the year would witness some of the most difficult combat to date before the onset of annual monsoon season began to greatly restrict air operations.

Although largely absent for the past year, VPAF's MiG-17s returned briefly to the skies in the spring to harass U.S. reconnaissance flights and to make fleeting efforts to engage strike forces. The results were about the same as in the past, with the VPAF downing a plane or two, but generally ending up on the receiving end. Between April 23 and May 12, for instance, Air Force F-4s shot down seven North Vietnamese fighters, including the first MiG-21, while suffering no losses in air-to-air engagements. The 555th TFS then based at Udorn would account for five of these seven enemy planes.[31] However, the VPAF, which now included almost two dozen MiG-21 fighters armed with Atoll air-to-air heat-seeking missiles, was far from finished.

During the second half of 1966, MiG fighters were attacking U.S. strike aircraft on average 12 times a month from the safety of their bases around Hanoi.[32] More important, they were becoming increasingly effective thanks to North Vietnamese ground controllers' growing understanding of American tactics, vulnerabilities of each aircraft type, route patterns, and mission procedures. MiG-17s tended to operate at low level and below U.S. radar coverage, before popping up to attack the American strike force from behind, while the supersonic and highly maneuverable MiG-21s would approach the U.S. formation head on and attack using air-to-air missiles or their 30-mm cannons. In mid-September the Air Force would lose its first two F-4s to MiGs. Sometimes the enemy fighter presence was enough to get American bombers to jettison their payloads short of their targets. From September to December, the Air Force calculated that 56 percent of their strike aircraft intercepted by MiGs were forced to dump their bombs prematurely and evade.[33] The VPAF did pay a price—losing six MiG-17s and two MiG-21s—but its pilots were also able to down seven American planes, including four fighters in air-to-air combat.[34]

Railroad and highway bridges were a high-priority target for American planes in the effort to disrupt, if not destroy, the transportation and supply network leading to and from Hanoi and Haiphong. Pictured here are several downed spans of the Dap Cau bridge over the Song Cau River about 15 miles northeast of Hanoi in July 1966. (Photo Naval History and Heritage Command)

Even in the face of continuing bombing restrictions and rising costs, Admiral Sharp and General McConnell pressed on by continuing to target the transportation and logistics infrastructure around Hanoi and Haiphong, as well in the southern panhandle. In mid-November the monthly sortie rate rose to 13,200, which was more than three and a half times the rate at the start of Rolling Thunder. Unfortunately, "the sortie rate" soon became the new metric by which McNamara's Pentagon began judging the success of the Air Force and the Navy in the bombing campaign. It not only needlessly stoked inter-service rivalry, but when combined with recurrent bombs shortages produced dangerous inefficiencies. Thus, it was not uncommon to deliberately increase the sortie rate by sending multiple planes on a strike with a couple of bombs rather than a single fully loaded aircraft or strike an insignificant target and risk plane and pilot for a very marginal return just to keep the sortie rate up.

There were of course still many significant targets in the heavily contested Hanoi–Haiphong route packages that also brought pilots into harm's way. The rail network to and from Hanoi in particular would require constant bombing to render it unserviceable. In the final months of the year the northwest rail line between Viet Tri and Yen Bai was under regular bombardment or overflown by armed recces, as was the northeast line between Bac Ninh and Bac Giang. Supply and ammo depots, railyards, military barracks, and smaller POL storage sites in the Hanoi–Haiphong area also came under repeated American air attacks even as rising numbers of MiG fighters, SA-2 missiles, and anti-aircraft rounds filled the air. Over the course of one ten-day-period (December 2–12) the Air Force and Navy would lose at total of 17 aircraft: eight to SA-2 missiles, six to anti-aircraft fire, and three shot down by fighters.[35] Ten pilots and crew were killed and nine other taken prisoner. Farther to the south, the USS *Coral Sea*'s CVW-2 suffered significant losses in the Vinh area, including the first loss to an SA-2 there. The Air Force too found the going tough in Route Pack I, especially around the heavily defended logistics hub of Dong Hoi.

"One had to always be looking for SAM lift-offs and keeping your head on a swivel" to avoid being shot down, because sometimes close was good enough for the 350-pound high-explosive warhead. (Photo National Museum of the U.S. Air Force)

By the time of the Christmas bombing pause, American pilots would have flown more than 79,000 sorties in 1966, including 280 B-52 strikes, and dropped over 100,000 tons of bombs on the North.[36] Combined Air Force and Navy aircraft losses since the start of Rolling Thunder now totaled 451 with Air Force F-105 squadrons suffering the worst combat losses, 111 planes in 1966 alone.[37] On the other side of the ledger American forces claimed to have destroyed or damaged nearly 5,500 vehicles, 13,600 military buildings, more than 3,400 bridges, and sunk at least 6,300 rivercraft of various types and sizes, as well as made more than 8,000 road cuts and nearly 900 rail line cuts.[38] In the process U.S. aircraft also destroyed or damaged some 1,200 anti-aircraft sites and 77 SAM sites.[39]

1967: Slugfest in the Skies

The new year dawned with both hope and frustration for the Americans. They could point to some successes in the level of damage they had inflicted on the North and the escalating price the North Vietnamese were paying for supporting the insurgency in South Vietnam. On the other hand, the administration's micromanagement of the air campaign bedeviled operational commanders, pilots, and air crews. Almost to a man they believed that if unleashed, air power could be the decisive factor in turning the tide of war. That belief, however, would never be tested. What would be tested in 1967 would be their mental toughness and perseverance to push forward with the status quo in the face a determined enemy that showed no signs of giving up.

Although heavily outnumbered and lacking the technological advantage of their American counterparts, the VPAF still posed a significant threat. Something had to be done. Unfortunately, despite repeated pleas for permission to take out the primary MiG bases around Hanoi, these airfields remained off limits. Administration officials were still too worried about the risk of provoking Moscow and Peking and drawing them directly into the war if their personnel were killed in any strike or if VPAF MiG operations were relocated to airfields in southern China.[40] Getting creative, the Americans came up with Operation Bolo to draw out the enemy MiGs.

As conceived Bolo was a classic ruse operation that turned North Vietnamese knowledge of existing Air Force tactics and mission patterns into an operational advantage for American fighter pilots. Flying a strike route into Route Pack VI A on the afternoon of January 2, 1967 and mimicking the formation, call signs, electronic signatures, and even the speed of an F-105 strike force, a disguised force of 28 F-4 Phantoms armed with radar-guided AIM-7 Sparrow missiles from the 8th TFW headed toward Hanoi. As Colonel Robin Olds, commander of the 8th and flying the lead, overflew the main MiG base at Phuc Yen he and his men awaited the anticipated arrival of attacking MiGs against their American "bomber force." Meanwhile, another force of 28 F-4s from the 366th TFW out of Da Nang would approach from the east coast to cover the airfields at Kep and Cat Bi should they react. Twenty-four F-105F Wild Weasels were also on hand to provide SAM suppression. The North Vietnamese took the bait and the fight was on. In the largest air-to-air engagement so far in the war—which ended up lasting only 15 minutes—pilots of the 8th TFW, known as "The Wolf Pack," shot down seven MiG-21s without suffering a loss. And four days later, two more MiG-21s were shot down by F-4s from the Wolf Pack's 355th TFS. Suffering the loss of nearly 50 percent of their most advanced fighters, the VPAF remained grounded for several months as it licked its wounds, regrouped, and refitted for the next round.

With the enemy fighter threat vastly diminished, the Air Force and Navy tried to make good use of the respite, but bad weather hampered operations over much of the northeast. Nonetheless, both services did their best to maintain the pressure. Armed recce missions repeatedly attacked segments of the northwest Hanoi–Lao Cai and northeast Hanoi–Lang Son rail lines, while larger missions were carried out against key highway and rail bridges in the Hanoi–Haiphong area, as well against the Viet Tri and Thai Nguyen thermal power plants outside the capital. Although North Vietnamese fighters were now largely absent, the heavy SAM and anti-aircraft defenses inflicted significant losses on U.S. aircraft. Six Air Force planes were downed by SA-2 missiles in January and February, along with another nine Air Force and Navy planes that were lost to enemy anti-aircraft fire.[41] The loss on February 4 of an Air Force EB-66 ECM aircraft north of Thai Nguyen was especially unnerving as the plane was struck by an SA-2 while flying at 30,000 feet and thus thought to be outside the range of the missiles.

To compensate for the lack of sorties in the northeast, air commanders increased missions in the far southern panhandle and along the central coast. While the Air Force concentrated on targets around Dong Hoi and infiltration routes north of the DMZ, naval aircraft from one of TF-77's four carriers focused their attention on the Ninh Binh–Thanh Hoa–Vinh corridor. Armed recce missions sought out road, rail, and waterway traffic both day and night in an effort to slow the flow of supplies southward. As usual bridges, ferry landings, and road bypasses were repeatedly hit to render them unserviceable. By early 1967 U.S. intelligence officials estimated that Hanoi was now relying on inland waterways and coastal shipping to move up to half of its supplies south of the 20th parallel.[42] In response the Navy began mining operations with six A-6 Intruders from the USS *Enterprise* sowing the first minefields in the Vinh and Dong Hoi river estuaries during the night of February 26.[43] Later in March, three more heavily trafficked estuaries from Thanh Hoa southward would also be mined by the Navy.

Too late. (Photo National Museum of the U.S. Air Force)

RF-4C Phantom on fire seconds after being hit by an SA-2 missile detonation, August 1967. Part one. (Photo National Museum of the U.S. Air Force)

RF-4C Phantom on fire and beginning to disintegrate following SA-2 missile detonation, August 1967. Part two. (Photo National Museum of the U.S. Air Force)

Augmented North Vietnamese air defenses in the southern panhandle, which now included SA-2 missiles as far south as Route Pack I, took their toll on the attackers; at least 11 American planes were shot down in the first two months of the year.[44] Two of these losses were an Air Force RF-101 Voodoo and a Navy RA-5 Vigilante flying high-speed, low-level, photo reconnaissance missions. Required to fly a fixed path at 300–500 feet above ground level, reconnaissance aircraft of all types were highly vulnerable to enemy ground fire. The American habit of overflying a target area immediately following a strike to assess battle damage also made them very predictable too. As dangerous as they were, Blue Tree photo recon missions were essential to collecting real-time intelligence and tactical information on the disposition of North Vietnamese defenses. Ultimately, dozens of aircrews would pay with their lives or end up as prisoners of war flying these often unheralded missions of the air campaign.

Improving weather over the northeast of the country beginning in March and a steadily expanding target list—including heretofore off-limits high-profile targets—upped the ante, as well as the intensity of combat over the skies of Hanoi and Haiphong as the air campaign moved toward its climax.

With improving weather over the northeast, the Air Force opened the next phase of an expanded bombing effort by launching a vigorous air assault with some 100 aircraft over the course of two days in early March against the huge Thai Nguyen industrial complex, located 35 miles due north of Hanoi. The critically important iron and steel works produced an estimate 300,000 tons of pig iron annually and was the only facility capable of producing prefabricated pontoon and bridge sections used to repair or replace bombed out bridges.[45] The complex also housed a thermal power plant, steel mill, and several assembly facilities. Although the neighboring railyard had been previously attacked, the plant itself had been off limits—until now. It would prove to be a tough nut to crack.

The opening round came on March 10 and, as the first wave of F-105s of the 355rd TFW out of Takhli, Thailand, closed on Thai Nguyen, a flight of four F-105F Wild Weasels raced ahead to soften up the enemy air defenses. One of the Wild Weasels was hit immediately by 85-mm anti-aircraft fire and crashed; both crew ejected safely and were captured. A second Wild Weasel had anti-aircraft fire punch a four-foot-diameter hole in its left wing and was forced to limp back to Takhli. Despite bullets filling the air and the arriving presence of MiG-21 fighters (which were making their first appearance in months), Captain Merlyn Dethlefsen and his wingman Major Ken Bell pressed home their attacks, avoiding both the worst of the flak and the attacking MiGs. Making four passes in their now flak-damaged aircraft, Dethlefsen and Bell fired their Shrike missiles, bombed, and strafed the Thai Nguyen SAM site until it was completely destroyed.[46] For his actions that day Captain Dethlefsen would be awarded the Congressional Medal of Honor, although he later said, "All I did was the job I was sent to do."[47]

Meanwhile, the F-105s along with several flights of F-4s were bombing the main complex with 750-pound bombs and inflicting heavy damage. Two Phantoms were seriously damaged by anti-aircraft fire during their runs, but both pilots were able to nurse their crippled aircraft just over the Laotian border before being forced to eject. All four crew members were successfully rescued. The 355th TFS returned the very next day to restrike the steel works and would pay a steep price again. Within the space of four minutes, two Thunderchiefs would be brought down by anti-aircraft fire and a third F-105 would fall to an SA-2 missile.[48] Although the strikes of March 10–11 heavily damaged the

Thai Nguyen facility and cut its production, they would cost the Air Force five airmen (one dead and four captured), six aircraft, and leave at least a dozen planes heavily damaged. And this was just the warm-up for what was to follow in the coming months.

While the Air Force had its hands full north of Hanoi, the Navy was ushering in a new era of aerial warfare just southeast of Thanh Hoa when it attacked the military barracks at Sam Son. On March 11, a single A-4 Skyhawk piloted by VA-212 skipper Homer Smith and escorted by F-4 fighters, took part in the first combat use of the 1,000-pound AGM-62 "Walleye" guided bomb.[49] The Walleye carried an 825-pound warhead and was equipped with television cameras that were able to lock onto any aiming point designated by the pilot. When released the "fire and forget" bomb would then glide to the target, allowing the pilot to release the bomb from a safer stand-off distance. Smith scored a direct hit with the bomb gliding straight through a window of the barracks before exploding inside.

The mission the next day would be more challenging: a Walleye strike against the infamous Thanh Hoa bridge. The plan called for three of VA-212's Skyhawks to make individual bombing runs, but target the exact same point. To their credit, all three pilots

A likely 57-mm round punched a hole in the wing of an F-105 out of Takhli, 1967. Although SAMs and MiGs were a near-constant threat, particularly as the air campaign moved into the heavily defended northeast, North Vietnamese anti-aircraft weapons and small arms took the highest toll on American planes. (Photo National Museum of the U.S. Air Force)

Air Force pilots inspect anti-aircraft damage to wing of an F-105 following a just-completed combat mission in 1967. (Photo National Museum of the U.S. Air Force)

placed their bombs within five feet of each other, rocking the bridge with nearly 2,500 pounds of explosives.[50] Yet when the smoke cleared the bridge still remained standing; the Dragon's Jaw would live on. Nonetheless, the new weapon had proved its worth and would go on to have a successful hit rate of over 95 percent.[51]

The coming months saw a marked U.S. escalation of daily raids and increased targeting of the North's strategic military and industrial heartland that included several targets within the Hanoi and Haiphong restricted zones. But this heartland was also the center of the North Vietnamese air defenses in the spring of 1967. Bristling with anti-aircraft weapons—now estimated at more than 7,000 in the country—and the heaviest concentration of SAM batteries in the country, many World War II-veteran pilots claimed it was better defended than Berlin. According to Colonel Olds, "The flak up north … is worse than Germany's because it is ten time more accurate [and] you get more thrown at you in a shorter span of time."[52] Toss in dozens of SA-2 missiles filling the air and the return of MiGs to the skies and it seemed that every mission was worse than the previous in this vortex of hell.

As dangerous as things were becoming in the northeast and especially around Hanoi, Admiral Sharp was not about to let this opportunity slip through his hands. On April 20 naval aircraft struck two thermal power plants in Haiphong. First a strike force of 36 aircraft from the USS *Kitty Hawk*'s CVW-11 struck Haiphong's main power plant, which was located only about a mile from the city center and within a heavily populated area. Thirteen A-4s loaded with 1,000-pound and 2,000-pound bombs delivered their ordnance precisely on the complex, knocking it off line; no bombs fell more than 200 feet outside the target, resulting in little to no damage to civilian housing.[53] Meanwhile planes from the USS *Ticonderoga* and *Bon Homme Richard* hit the second plant on the western outskirts causing significant damage to the facility. No aircraft were lost and Skyhawk Iron Hands claimed to have knocked out three SAM sites during the attacks.

A few days later on April 24 the Americans launched their first, and long-awaited, strikes on North Vietnamese airfields at Kep and Hoa Loc, northeast of Hanoi. An initial daytime strike against Kep by CVW-11's A-4s was followed by a nighttime attack by the wing's A-6s, leaving the airfield and much of its air defenses damaged. An accompanying attack by eight Air Force F-105s of the 333rd TFS against Hoa Loc was likewise deemed a major success with the Redleg Lancers claiming to have destroyed over a dozen MiGs on the ground while suffering no losses.[54] The Navy did lose two planes to anti-aircraft fire over Kep, but Phantoms from VF-114 also bagged two MiG-17s during the raid.[55] Kep and Hoa Loc, as well as other MiG bases outside Haiphong and Hanoi, would be hit repeatedly throughout the rest of April and into May. During one such mission on May 1 a Skyhawk flown by Lieutenant Commander Theodore Swartz of VA-76 shot down a MiG-17 over Kep with 20-mm cannon fire and 5-inch Zuni rockets, the only MiG fighter downed by an A-4 during the war.[56]

There was, however, a price to be paid as the events of April 30 showed when a strike package of the 355th TFS was jumped by MiG-21 fighters west of Hanoi. In the ensuing action an F-105F Wild Weasel and then two other strike Thunderchiefs were downed by the MiGs using their Atoll air-to-air missiles. Another F-105 was also badly damaged, but managed to escape back to Thailand. An attempt to rescue the downed fliers had to be called off when one of the A-1s flying rescue cover was nearly shot down by ground fire and a rescue helicopter developed mechanical problems and had to abort. All four of the pilots and crew survived their ejections, but were taken prisoner.[57] Likewise, multiple raids against railyards, barracks, ammunition and vehicle depots, and POL storage facilities on the outskirts of Hanoi by the Air Force and against Haiphong by the Navy proved costly, losing one or two aircraft on nearly every mission. By mid-May the Americans had lost at least 25 planes to anti-aircraft fire or SAMs, resulting in 15 dead and 12 taken prisoner.[58]

The raids also resulted in the largest aerial battles so far in the war. On May 13 two groups of MiG-17s pounced on F-105s of the 354th TFS as they were re-striking the Yen Viet railyard. When it was all over five MiGs had been blasted from the skies—three by 20-mm cannon fire and two by Sidewinder air-to-air missiles—without the loss of a single American fighter.[59] Earlier in the day, other Air Force F-4 pilots downed two MiG-17s, bringing the day's tally to seven. The very next day, Da Nang F-4s of the 480th TFS shot down three more MiG-17s over the northeast that brought the total to ten enemy planes destroyed in two days.[60]

The Navy got into the action over Hanoi in dramatic fashion on May 19 when it was tasked with knocking out the city's main downtown thermal power plant. It was also the day the North was celebrating the birthday of Ho Chi Minh and would be a day to remember. A flight of two VA-212 Skyhawks armed with 1,000-pound Walleye guide bombs and led once again by Commander Homer Smith, accompanied by 12 of the *Bon Homme Richard*'s F-8 Crusaders (six flying escort and six for flak suppression) and two sections of A-4 Iron Hands, made a beeline for the center of Hanoi. Earlier in the day a large diversionary alpha strike was launched against the Van Dien military vehicle

Navy pilots from the USS *Midway*'s VF-21 in their F-4B Phantoms scored the first MiG kills of the war on June 17, 1965 when they shot down two MiG-17s north of Thanh Hoa. (Photo Emil Buehler Library, National Naval Aviation Museum)

MiG-17 pilots listen to a discussion of dogfighting tactics. VPAF pilots made good use of the American penchant for standardized routines and predictable tactics to often gain the upper hand in their initial attacks. (Photo National Museum of the U.S. Air Force)

Post-combat debrief: an Air
Force fighter pilot recounts
how he got the best of an
enemy MiG fighter. (Photo
National Museum of the
U.S. Air Force)

park and SAM support depot on the southern outskirts of Hanoi by planes from the USS
Enterprise and *Kitty Hawk*. Both strikes faced heavy resistance in the form of anti-aircraft
barrages and SA-2 missiles, as well as the presence of hastily scrambled MiG-17 fighters.
Unfortunately, the Walleyes were dropped at too low an altitude to reach the target.

Undeterred, the Navy returned again on May 21 and this time the Walleye-equipped
A-4s scored a direct hit on the plant.[61] After losing two F-8s to a combination of anti-aircraft
fire and SA-2s during the run-in, the departing strike force became entangled in one of the
largest air-to-air battles of the war when a force of ten MiG-17s converged on the American
planes. In the ensuing chaos in the skies east of Hanoi, VF-24 and VF-211 Crusader pilots
were able to gain the upper hand and shot down four of the MiGs without the strike force
suffering any further losses. It was not all bad news for the North Vietnamese. Their air
defenses that Friday cost the Navy six planes and ten aviators, one dead and nine captured
(although three of these POWs would die shortly after their capture). These losses when
combined with the further shooting down of a Marine F-8 by ground fire north of the DMZ
would be the single worst day of the war for the Navy so far.[62]

The following day, the VPAF once again took to the skies to contest an Air Force
F-105 strike on targets near Kep. While still east of Kep, the formation that was
escorted by F-4s of the 433rd TFS and led by air wing commander Colonel Olds was
jumped by two groups of fast, attacking MiG-17s. One F-4 was hit immediately and
disintegrated into a ball of flames. The 433rd pilots, however, got their revenge in
the twisting and turning dogfight by bagging six of the attackers.[63] A couple of days
later, Air Force Phantoms out of Da Nang shot down two MiG-21s, which brought
the monthly total of enemy fighters destroyed by Air Force pilots to 20 in 72 aerial
engagements.[64] The Navy added another six to the North Vietnamese loss column,
making May the worse month of the war for the VPAF. Since the start of the year the
VPAF had lost at least 50 planes, including 15 advanced MiG-21s, in air-to-air combat
with their American counterparts.[65]

Right: As commander of the 8th TFW at Ubon, Thailand from September 1966 to December 1967, Colonel Robin Olds sought to boost morale and instill confidence in his pilots through his aggressive—but not always welcomed at higher command levels—tactics and leadership style. Under his command F-4 Wolf Pack pilots tallied 24 MiG kills; four were by Olds.

Below: Colonel Robin Olds (top left) with fellow F-4 pilots of the 555th TFS, "Triple Nickel," following a successful mission in early May 1967. (Photo National Museum of the U.S. Air Force)

Above and Beyond: Battling the SAMs

In advance of an April 19, 1967 strike against the barracks at Xuan Mai southwest of Hanoi, a flight of four F-105F Wild Weasels from the 355th TFW was preparing to attack two of the defending SAM sites when they were suddenly intercepted by a swarm of MiG-17 fighters. One F-105F was quickly shot down and two others were seriously damaged and had to escape back to Thailand. With the last remaining Wild Weasel piloted by Major Leo Thorsness circling the downed crew and attempting to coordinate a rescue attempt, a MiG-17 flashed in front of him. Maneuvering wildly while giving chase, Thorsness was able to shoot down the enemy fighter with his 20-mm cannons. Now running low on fuel, he left the scene to refuel with a nearby KC-135 tanker before returning to the rescue operation.

Upon returning Thorsness quickly found himself facing several remaining MiGs that were threatening the arriving rescue aircraft. One of the A-1s was hit by 37-mm cannon fire and crashed into a mountainside. While playing cat and mouse with remaining enemy fighters to distract them from the remaining A-1, Thorsness was able to damage another MiG-17 before running out of ammunition. Now critically low on fuel and unable to refuel with the KC-135, because he allowed another F-105 to take on fuel to avoid flaming out, Thorsness headed for Thailand. He barely made it, touching down at Udorn with his just fumes in his tank. Although newly arriving F-105 escorts were able to engage and shoot down three more MiGs using Sidewinder missiles, the rescue attempt had to be abandoned and the downed Wild Weasel crew was taken prisoner. For his actions, Major Thorsness was awarded the Medal of Honor.

The next day over the skies near Haiphong Lieutenant Commander Michael Estocin of VA-192 was one of three A-4 pilots flying an Iron Hand mission during a strike on two thermal power plants near the city. With two SAM sites already damaged by the Iron Hands, Estocin pressed his attack on the third site despite having suffered considerable damage to his aircraft from a near miss of an SA-2 missile. Streaming fuel from his damaged plane and with just minutes to spare, he linked up with a KA-3 tanker over the Gulf of Tonkin. Unfortunately, the A-4 was losing fuel nearly as fast as it was taking it on, thus forcing Estocin to remain connected to the tanker as the pair made for the USS *Ticonderoga*. With the carrier in sight, he unplugged from the tanker with only enough fuel for one landing attempt. After making a controlled crash landing, the burning plane was immediately covered in foam by firefighters. Estocin walked away.

Six days later, on April 26, 1967, Estocin was flying another Iron Hand mission in support of a strike on a POL tank farm near Haiphong. Orbiting overhead at 12,000 feet Estocin waited for the SAM batteries to activate, but they remained quiet and failed to engage the attacking planes. However, just as the aircraft were departing the target several SA-2 missiles were launched in Estocin's direction. He dove, turning into an approaching missile, but apparently misjudged his break away or waited too long and the exploding warhead sent shrapnel tearing into his Skyhawk. The burning plane began to spin wildly, shedding pieces before somehow Estocin righted and leveled the aircraft off at 2,000 feet. An accompanying F-8 was unable to raise a response over the radio and closed in to see the pilot slumped over in the shattered cockpit. Soon after the disintegrating A-4 rolled inverted, the Shrike missiles fired off from the heat, and the plane dove into the ground. For his actions on April 20 and 26, Michael Estocin was posthumously awarded the Medal of Honor.

Safe at last. Both Air Force and the Navy search and rescue teams went to great lengths and put themselves in harm's way to rescue downed pilots and crewmen before they fell into enemy hands. (Photo National Museum of the U.S. Air Force)

A wounded Lieutenant Colonel James Lindberg-Hughes, an F-105D pilot with the 469th TFS out of Korat, is paraded through the streets following his capture near Hanoi on May 5, 1967. Hughes like his fellow pilots would be labeled "an air pirate" and subject to repeated bouts of torture at the Hanoi Hilton. He was released in March 1973.

Hoa Lo prison, nicknamed the "Hanoi Hilton" by American flyers, was a former French colonial prison that by the end of the war housed several hundred U.S. prisoners-of-war, including Everett Alvarez, John McCain, George Day, Robbie Risner, Jerimiah Denton, and James Stockdale.

The Bombing Debate Redux

Just as the bombing campaign appeared to making headway, divided opinion within the administration over its effectiveness and, more importantly, over its future once again came to the fore. The divide was especially stark between the civilian and the uniformed leadership in the Pentagon. Precipitating the reinvigorated debate was Westmoreland's April request for an additional 100,000 more American ground troops and the broader question of the strategic direction of the war—and by implication of the role of the air campaign.

McNamara had become increasingly pessimistic over the direction of war in general and, in particular, viewed the bombing of the North as unsuccessful.[66] The North still showed no sign of buckling after more than two years of American bombing and, if anything, McNamara believed the bombing might have hardened Hanoi's resolve. Moreover, critics of the air campaign saw few significant targets left to attack and those that did remain did not warrant the loss of men and aircraft or antagonizing the Soviets or Chinese. There was also a huge international political risk to the United States of escalating the bombing further. "The picture of the world's greatest superpower killing or seriously injuring 1,000 noncombatants a week, while trying to pound a tiny, backward nation into submission on an issue whose merits are hotly debated is not a pretty one," wrote McNamara to the President in May.[67]

Thus, by the summer of 1967 the Secretary and several of his senior civilian deputies began advocating for a de-escalation of the war. It was also a point of no return for

McNamara. He was now convinced that outright military victory in Vietnam was unobtainable and that the administration "should seek a lesser political objective through negotiations."[68] He resisted Westmoreland's troop request and proposed cutting back the bombing to below the 20th parallel with an emphasis on slowing the flow of supplies and men southward. The so-called "doves" within the administration were in essence opting for a defensive strategy that focused on containing the Viet Cong insurgency and thereby denying it and the North the victory they were seeking. Rolling Thunder would become a limited interdiction campaign, a sideshow to the war.

Not surprisingly, McNamara's proposed new course of action did not sit well with the Joint Chiefs and Admiral Sharp, who were still bent on prosecuting the war to its fullest and defeating northern aggression. Chairman Earle Wheeler characterized McNamara's proposed de-escalation, as "an aerial Dien Bien Phu."[69] Sharp pointed to positive developments in the air campaign—heavy MiG loses, damaged airfields, less effective SAM firings thanks to U.S. countermeasures, and major damage to infrastructure—and the need to maintain the momentum in the northeast. He also emphasized that more still had to be done, citing the lack of authorization to strike key targets in restricted and prohibited zones and the need to diversify attacks rather than concentrate on a single system (such as transportation) to gain an operational advantage.[70] Secretary of State Rusk, likewise, warned that America's credibility was at stake and it made no sense "to stop half of the war," while Hanoi continued to have a free hand in fueling the violence in the South.[71]

With an administration increasingly divided over the direction of not only the air campaign, but the war in general, President Johnson sought to steer a middle course. The White House released 16 additional targets in the northeast—including six within the restricted zones of Hanoi and Haiphong—in an effort to placate the hawks and preempt Congressional calls for increased bombing of the North. At the same time he rebuffed Wheeler's and Sharp's call for a dramatically expanded strategic bombing campaign, which he believed would draw the Soviets and Chinese directly into the war. Most important of all, Johnson became convinced "that bombing [of the North] was less important to a successful outcome in Vietnam than what was done militarily on the ground in the South."[72] In somewhat a pyrrhic victory for McNamara, Johnson thus implicitly validated the defeat of the southern insurgency as the cornerstone of American war strategy.

Following McNamara's public testimony before Senate Armed Service committee members in early August, where he openly questioned the effectiveness of the bombing campaign and dismissed calls for a new air campaign as "completely illusory" and "futile," his days were numbered.[73] Now a public lightning rod for military and Congressional frustration over the failure of the air campaign to bring Hanoi to heel and Johnson's loss of confidence in his leadership of the Pentagon, McNamara would be replaced by Clark Clifford in November. McNamara's efforts to advance U.S. goals in Vietnam based on quantifiable metrics and through a tightly controlled and cost-effective manner proved unrealistic and unworkable; the chaos of war simply doesn't work that way. As for the air campaign, it would continue to play itself out as a mash-up of coercive diplomacy, strategic bombing, and interdiction that satisfied none of the objectives of all three strategies.

6. ONCE MORE INTO THE BREACH

While the future of Rolling Thunder hung in the balance as the debate over the bombing intensified back in Washington in the summer of 1967, Admiral Sharp sought to make the best of the existing situation and the favorable weather to tighten the air ring around Hanoi and Haiphong. Even if most key targets in the prohibited and restricted zones still remained off limits to attack—59 percent of the military facilities and 70 percent of the transportation targets[1]—Sharp was determined to do his best to isolate both cities from the rest of the country. This would require him to unleash the largest sustained air assault on the North and it would produce the greatest American losses of the air campaign. It might also just possibly turn the tide of the war.

Despite past setbacks and wavering faith in the bombing effort back in Washington, there was indeed reason for optimism among American air commanders. By the early summer, the bombing was credited with having destroyed 86 percent of the North's electrical power capacity, 40 percent of its major military installations north of 20th parallel, and of disrupting up to half of the country's war-supporting industry. It was estimated that 30 percent of supplies and war matériel destined for Hanoi were now being destroyed en route. In addition, at least 81 MiG fighters had been shot down or destroyed on the ground since the start of the year and three VPAF air bases had been rendered inoperable.[2] Nonetheless, Sharp warned that "the job yet to be done was significant," as he continued to push for a more aggressive, less restricted strategic bombing campaign, one that was capable of "bringing the war to a successful, early conclusion."[3] He didn't get his wish. The White House instead opted for largely maintaining the status quo with a tightly controlled release of new targets as circumstances warranted. Time, however, was running out for the Americans.

The Slugfest Continues

Fighting the war he had, rather than the war he wanted, Sharp sought to ratchet up the pressure on Hanoi and Haiphong through intense round the clock bombing. Although lines of communication and supply links to China received special attention, the renewed air offensive saw the most encompassing strategic bombing effort to date. In addition to stepping up attacks on the transportation network in the northeast, industrial and military targets found themselves under heavy assault too, as did the Thanh Hoa–Vinh corridor and shipping along the central coastline. June would see a near record high of more than 11,000 Rolling Thunder sorties flown.[4] To keep the enemy off balance and improve the effectiveness of the American strikes, North Vietnamese air defenses and MiG airfields (with the notable exception of the MiG-21 base at Phuc Yen and the Gia Lam international airport) were hit repeatedly.

Throughout the summer Air Force planes continued to hammer road and rail links into and out of Hanoi, knocking down key rail and highway bridges almost as quickly as they were repaired. Meanwhile, the Navy kept up its efforts to isolate Haiphong by targeting the city's four main bridges leading to the port. Other priority transportation targets included railyards and rolling stock, the vital Hai Duong bridge midway between

Haiphong and Hanoi, and stranded trains and truck convoys caught out in the open. The area around Kep on the Hanoi–Long Son rail corridor was the focus of intense Air Force F-105 strikes through June and July. It was also one of the most heavily defended corridors, housing an array of anti-aircraft weaponry, which included 85-mm radar control guns that could take down an aircraft at 15,000 feet. During one particularly bad day in early July, three Thunderchiefs were shot down by anti-aircraft fire in the space of four minutes.[5]

Navy pilots were also learning that there were no easy missions over the northeast in the summer of 1967. While they were inflicting significant damage on key transportation targets, such as dropping multiple spans of the Kien An highway bridge south of Haiphong and the heavily damaging the Hai Duong bridge and railyard to the west of the city, these results came with the loss of at least one plane per mission. During strikes on July 18–19 against the well-defended Co Trai rail bridge some 20 miles south of Hanoi, the USS *Oriskany*'s air wing would lose three A-4s—all from the same squadron, The Saints of VA-164—and one F-8. These losses were further compounded when a rescue helicopter from the USS *Hornet* was also shot down, killing the crew of four.[6] Things would get even worse for the men of CVW-16 or "Bloody 16," as it came to be known. Before the *Oriskany* left Yankee Station in January 1968 following 122 days on the line, CVW-16 would lose 29 planes in combat and ten more in operational accidents. Eleven pilots would be dead and another eight marched into captivity.[7]

With the early August release by the White House of 20 more high-value targets, the pace and intensity of air campaign further quickened. More important, several of the new targets fell within the prohibited zone of Hanoi, one of which was the Paul Doumer bridge. A prominent symbol of French colonialism that was completed in 1902, the mile-long rail and highway bridge spanned the Red River linking downtown Hanoi with its eastern districts. The bridge's main central train track was flanked on each side by road bridges making it an imposing structure. Critically, it was the only rail link to Haiphong and the only rail crossing of the Red River within 30 miles for southbound traffic out of the capital. American intelligence estimated that 26 trains carrying 6,000 tons of cargo crossed the bridge each day and it was also thought to be surrounded by more than a hundred anti-aircraft guns ranging up to 100-mm and ringed by multiple nearby SAM sites.[8]

General William Momyer, now commander of the Seventh Air Force, was bent on attacking on the bridge as soon as possible, so a previously scheduled mission by the 355th TFW on August 11 was scrubbed and planes were diverted to the new mission. Forced to rearm all of the strike F-105s now with 3,000-pound bombs, the ground crews of the 355th worked feverishly to accomplish the task and meet   General William Momyer the afternoon launch time. A little after 2 p.m. Colonel Bob White, the wing's deputy commander, led the strike force of 20 F-105s toward Hanoi and the Paul Doumer bridge. The Takhli Thunderchiefs were accompanied by four F-105F Wild Weasels and another four F-105s as flak suppressors. Trailing White's formation was an identical one from Korat, as well as F-4s from Ubon carrying bomb loads, while still other Wolf Pack Phantoms provided fighter cover for the mission.[9]

After refueling over Laos, the powerful strike force made a beeline for Hanoi. About 30 miles from the city, multiple SAM sites began to come on line, so the Wild Weasels went to work. Several sites were quickly hit and silenced, yet at least a half dozen SA 2 missiles streaked skyward at the Americans. White pressed on. Suddenly a flight of four fast-approaching MiGs closed on the lead formation, but to everyone's relief then streaked past without firing. Now approaching the target, the North Vietnamese unleashed a heavy barrage of anti-aircraft fire as the first Thunderchiefs rolled in through the flak to drop their M118 3,000-pound bombs at 8,000 feet. Colonel Robin Olds and his F-4 flight followed suit. Soon nearly 100 tons of ordnance had rained down on the Paul Doumer bridge, leaving behind the demolished center span of the rail bridge in the water and destroying sections of both road bridges. Hanoi's rail link to Haiphong was no more. Surprisingly, only two planes were badly damaged, but managed to return to their bases. A follow-up strike the next day inflicted additional damage with the loss of one F-105D. For their efforts, White, Olds, and three other Air Force personnel would all be awarded the Air Force Cross, the second highest decoration for bravery.[10]

The Navy had a go at its own high-profile target on August 21 when six A-4s equipped with Walleye guide bombs from The Saints of VA-163 flying off the *Oriskany* struck Hanoi's downtown thermal power plant. This was the same plant that was first damaged back in May, but had been since repaired and was back on line. The strike plan called for a daring attack from six different angles with all six Skyhawks launching

The last half of 1967 saw the air campaign in the northeast intensify as Admiral Sharp sought to isolate Hanoi and Haiphong from the rest of the country. (U.S. Navy photo)

their Walleyes simultaneously within 15–20 miles of the target in the hope that they would obtain at least four direct hits.[11] Moreover, to maintain a low profile there would be no Iron Hand, no flak suppression or fighter cover directly accompanying the strike. The pilots would be on their own deep in enemy territory. As Commander Bryan Compton and his men approached the target the North Vietnamese fired 20–30 SA-2 missiles at the attackers and let loose with a stream of anti-aircraft fire. Two Skyhawks were severely damaged by exploding 57-mm and 85-mm shells, forcing Lieutenant Commander Dean Cramer in his badly damaged jet, now holed, on fire, and leaking fuel to abort.[12] The remaining pilots, including Lieutenant Commander Jim Busey in his badly shot-up aircraft, pressed on and delivered their payloads on target. All five scored hits, with three striking the main generator facility and two the boiler house.[13] Both Cramer and Busey barely made it back to the ship with minutes to spare as their crippled aircraft were on the verge of disintegrating. Busey's A-4 had 125 holes in the starboard wing alone, including an 8x14-inch one, and had its starboard stabilizer and elevator shot out. Cramer's plane had over a hundred holes in it.[14] All The Saints pilots would receive medals for the successful mission that day; both Compton and Busey were awarded the Navy Cross.

View from an A-4 Skyhawk as it begins its bombing run, while the lead Skyhawk pulls away from the target having just delivered its payload. (Photo Emil Buehler Library, National Naval Aviation Museum)

As successful as the strike on Hanoi's main power plant was on the 21st, the North Vietnamese defenders made the American pay elsewhere by downing six U.S. aircraft that day, which resulted in the deaths of five airmen and the capture of three others.[15] The USS *Constellation*'s CVW-14 would bear the burden, losing four planes. First an F-4 flying a flak suppression mission for a morning raid on a highway bridge near Uong Bi, just north of Haiphong, was fatally hit by anti-aircraft fire forcing the crew to eject. Then later that morning four A-6s from VA-196 struck the Duc Noi railyard five miles northeast of Hanoi in the face of strong air defenses. One Intruder had its wing taken off by an SA-2 missile detonation, one of more than 50 missiles fired at CVW-14 aircraft that day. Following the strike, two of the Intruders became separated from the strike force and mistakenly flew northeast into Chinese airspace where they were shot down by Chinese MiG-19s. One crew member survived and was held captive in China until his release in March 1973 following the Paris Peace Accords. As the Navy was attacking Duc Noi, F-105s out of Takhli were bombing the Yen Vinh railyard northwest of Hanoi. Two Thunderchiefs fell to anti-aircraft fire during the raid and both pilots were killed.[16]

Things got even worse two days later. An 18-plane alpha strike on the recently repaired Bac Giang rail and highway bridge, 25 miles northeast of the city, led to the loss of an F-105D on a flak suppression mission; a similar fate befell a Navy Phantom just east of Hanoi when it was hit by an SA-2 missile and erupted in a ball of flame. The rail network northwest of Hanoi was also subject to heavy bombing with the rail marshalling yard at Yen Vien just outside Hanoi being targeted on the August 23 by F-4s out of Ubon and F-105s out of Takhli. While making final preparations for their run-in on the target, a flight of low-flying MiG-21s broken into the strike formation in an effort to disrupt the raid. In the ensuing dogfight, two Phantoms flying cover from the 555th TFS or "Triple Nickel" were downed by Atoll missiles. As the MiGs and Phantom escorts battled it out, the rest of the strike force pressed on to the target only to be greeted with a hail of anti-aircraft fire. One F-4D was shot down immediately and another fatally crippled, barely making it across the Laotian border before the crew was forced to eject. To make matter worse, several F-105s were jumped by MiG-17s after finishing their bombing runs, which precipitated another dogfight over the capital's western suburbs. This time the Americans got the best of the VPAF by shooting down three of the MiG-17s with 20-mm cannon fire.[17] The day's tally: six American planes lost, four dead, and five captured against the North Vietnamese loss of three planes.

Not only were the MiGs once again becoming more aggressive and effective, but so too were the SAM batteries. In the month of August alone, Navy pilots reported nearly 200 missile sightings and would lose six planes to SA-2s.[18] Three of these losses were A-4s of CVW-16 that were shot out of the sky at 16,000 feet as they flew a mission against the Vat Cach Thuong rail bridge near Haiphong on the last day of the month.[19] A total of 39 aircraft—23 Air Force and 16 Navy—were lost in August, bringing the total of U.S. aircraft lost over North Vietnam to 649 since the start of Rolling Thunder.[20] Throughout the autumn the loss rate would continue to steadily climb; "We were losing men and airplanes at an alarming rate," recalled an Air Force pilot with the 345th TFS. Eight of 15 of his fellow F-105 pilots had been shot down within months of their arrival at Takhli.[21]

September and early October saw a pullback of attacks within Hanoi's prohibited zone in response to the opening of a potential peace channel in Paris. Strikes elsewhere in the northeast, however, continued as efforts to isolate Haiphong and create a supply

Thai Nguyen iron and steel plant under attack in the spring of 1967; attacking the North's economic infrastructure became a growing priority in 1967. (Photo National Museum of the U.S. Air Force)

bottleneck at the port intensified. Although still denied authorization to close the harbor with aerial mining, Sharp launched an all-out assault on the four main rail and highway bridges leading to and from the city. They were hit repeatedly to keep them out of service. Likewise, ferries, railyards, shuttle barges, and even the harbor dredgers were struck. By October the port had a backlog of some 200,000 tons of supplies and the amount of time to unload arriving freighters had more than doubled.[22]

With the North Vietnamese once again rebuffing the latest American peace talk overtures, Johnson again resorted to the stick by opening up the target list in October. The port of Cam Pha just northeast of Haiphong was struck and, more importantly, the main MiG-21 fighter base at Phuc Yen was heavily bombed for the first time on October 24. This air strike would be the first of several over the course of the next three days. Phuc Yen along with Kep and Cat Bi, outside Haiphong, would be temporarily put out of action and at least 20 VPAF aircraft were destroyed on the ground.[23] Four Navy and two Air Force planes were shot down by a combination of anti-aircraft fire and SA-2 missiles during the raids.[24] In a break from the past, all MiG airfields (with the exception of Hanoi's Gia Lam international airport) were now repeatedly attacked over the next several months, Phuc Yen itself at least another half dozen times. This ultimately, forced the VPAF to relocate its fighters to the safety of Gia Lam airfield or to bases in southern China by the end of the year.

Damaged Haiphong power plant, April 1967. (Photo Emil Buehler Library, National Naval Aviation Museum)

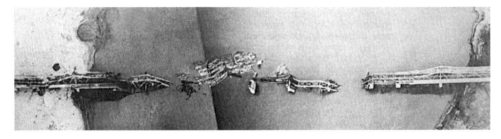

Hanoi's critical Paul Doumer bridge lies in ruins following a large F-105 strike in August 1967. (Photo National Museum of the U.S. Air Force)

With major restrictions now lifted, critical targets within Hanoi's prohibited zone once again were subject to the American wrath. The now-repaired Paul Doumer bridge was hit on October 25 by 21 F-105s from the 355th TFW using 63 tons of 3,000-pound bombs, which collapsed two spans into the Red River.[25] Two days later Hanoi's other main bridge over the Canal des Rapides just northeast of the city was heavily damaged by F-105s from Korat and Takhli, but SA-2 missiles downed two Thunderchiefs during the raid. A third plane, an F-4D flying combat air patrol was also shot down by enemy anti-aircraft fire.[26] For good measure follow-up strikes over the next several days inflicted additional damage on both bridges.

Hanoi's power infrastructure was also targeted again with several raids against the city's thermal power plants. During one raid on October 26, an A-4 flown by Lieutenant Commander John McCain was one of two CVW-16 planes knocked out the sky by SA-2 missiles. Badly injured, McCain landed in a downtown Hanoi lake where he almost drowned before being captured. (After his release and retirement, McCain went on to a prominent career in American politics starting in the early 1980s.) Aircraft from the *Constellation* also had a go at the infamous Thanh Hoa bridge at the end of the month, but with the same lackluster results. The Dragon's Jaw continued to be a thorn in the Americans' side. An encounter between the accompanying F-4 escorts and four MiG-17s left one Phantom so badly damage that it was forced to ditch alongside the *Constellation*.[27]

Determine to press the advantage as long as possible, Admiral Sharp and General Momyer pushed their men and equipment to the limit in the final months of the year and into early 1968. With four full carrier air wings and three tactical fighter wings plus a large number of supporting aircraft in South Vietnam and Thailand, the array of American air power was indeed formidable. Burdensome rules of engagement, White House micromanagement, and political calculations still hampered their efforts, but there was still a sense of optimism by American military leaders that the North Vietnamese might be nearing a tipping point. But they also knew that time was running out and the window of opportunity closing fast.

The North Vietnamese, however, weren't ready to capitulate. To be sure Hanoi's air defenses had been battered—64 MiGs had been lost since the spring, it had expended more than 3,000 surface-to-air missiles, and had seen thousands of anti-aircraft weapons destroyed—and its airfields had suffered relentless bombardment at the hands of the Americans. Thousands of trucks, rail cars, and watercraft of all sizes had been destroyed since the start of the air campaign, as had tens of thousands of tons of supplies and military equipment destined for the South. Large portions of the North's industrial and power infrastructure lay in ruins. The country's ravaged transportation network now consisted of a patchwork of hastily repaired bridges and rail lines, improvised bypasses or temporary structures that were held together by the sheer doggedness of nearly half a million laborers. Nonetheless, Hanoi was determined to outlast the Americans by staying the course, because it remained confident that victory on the battlefield in the South was within its grasp and just a matter of time.

Despite their losses, the North Vietnamese still had plenty of fight left in them as the Americans were to soon find out. Deteriorating weather over the northeast at the end of the year reduced operations there, but Sharp did his best to maintain the momentum of the air campaign. The primary MiG-21 base at Phu Yen airfield was subject to continual harassing attacks, as were the other VPAF bases at Kep, Kein An, and Hoa Loc throughout

The White House finally gave permission to begin striking the primary MiG-21 base at Phuc Yen northwest of Hanoi in October 1967, which ushered in several months of intense air-to-air combat. (Photo National Museum of the U.S. Air Force)

November and December that rendered them all inoperable at times. Key rail and highway bridges in and around Hanoi and Haiphong once again were heavily bombed as isolation efforts on these two cities continued.

The attacks, however, often came at a steep price. For example, a November 18 raid on Phu Yen by the 388th TFW out of Korat ended in disaster with the loss of four of the sixteen F-105 in the attack. The formation was first jumped by a flight of MiG-21s that were quickly able to shoot down two Thunderchiefs (one of which was a Wild Weasel) with their Atoll missiles. Once over the target the SAM batteries were able to down two more of the attackers. Four airmen were killed, including Colonel Edward Burdett, the wing commander of the 388th who was leading the mission. The following day a 20-plane Navy strike against Haiphong's bridges and airfields was engaged by four MiG-17s

A-6 pilots from VA-165 aboard the USS *Ranger* inspect their MK-82 Snakeye bomb loads prior to a mission, January 1968. (Photo Emil Buehler Library, National Naval Aviation Museum)

forward deployed at Kien An airfield. In the ensuing dogfight with the VF-151 Phantom escorts, pilots of the VPAF's 923rd Fighter Regiment were able to shoot down two of the F-4s and escape without loss.[28] To add to that day's deadly toll, the Air Force would also lose four more aircraft to SA-2 missiles on missions around Hanoi in a day that saw nearly 100 missile launches.[29]

Despite the weather conditions that would greatly limit operations in the northeast, mid-December saw several notable engagements and successes for both sides. Hanoi's Canal des Rapides and Paul Doumer bridges were once again struck in mid-month. Both were heavily damaged, with the latter having five connective spans destroyed that effectively cut off direct rail traffic to the east until April 1968 when a bypass pontoon rail bridge was completed.[30] While the battle of Hanoi and Haiphong bridges continued to play out in late 1967, the aerial battle for the control of skies intensified too. The period from December 14–19 saw multiple dogfights involving dozens of planes. The Navy drew first blood on the 14th when a flight of four MiG-17s tried to pounce on an A-4 Iron Hand mission near Haiphong, but they soon found themselves grappling with the escorting F-8s. Three of the MiGs broke off, but the fourth remained to engage in a weaving dogfight with the Crusaders that extended down to near ground level at times before it was shot down. The VPAF got their revenge a few days later. First, a MiG-21 shot down an F-4D over Kep following another raid on the airfield on December 16. Then the next day, a coordinated attack by MiG-21s and MiG-17s intercepted a 32-plane Air Force strike against a rail bridge north of Yen Bai. The MiG-21s broke into the F-105 formation, downing one

Left: Often as quickly as the Americans knocked down a bridge (center), the North Vietnamese found creative ways to repair the damage or build bypass routes (top). (Photo National Museum of the U.S. Air Force)

Below: The 14th TRS out of Udorn, Thailand performed yeoman service throughout the war flying combat reconnaissance missions. (Photo National Museum of the U.S. Air Force)

with an Atoll air-to-air missile, while the MiG-17s engaged the F-4 escorts. Gaining the initial advantage the MiGs were able to unleash a fusillade of 23-mm and 37-mm cannon fire that engulfed one of the Phantoms in flames.[31] Wild Weasels from the 355th TFW out of Takhli evened the score on December 19 during a chaotic mêlée between MiG-17s, F-4s, and F-105s when they were able to gain position on two of the attacking MiGs and down them with 20-mm cannon fire.[32]

Although only two American aircraft fell to SA-2 missiles in December, one of those lost was a newly arrived A-7A Corsair II from VA-147 off the USS *Ranger* on the 22nd. The new planes represented the future of Navy light attack aircraft with their advanced avionics, although these systems would not be fully developed until the production of the E model in early 1969.[33] When paired together with increasing numbers of A-6s, the A-7s had the potential to decisively tip the scales in the Americans favor. The only question was, would there be enough time? By the end of the year the United States had lost another 326 aircraft—113 of which were F-105s—thus bringing total loses for the air campaign to almost 800.[34] In return American pilots had shot down 89 MiG fighters and inflicted an estimated $370 million in damage to the North Vietnamese economy.[35]

Fire at Sea

While conducting combat operations off the coast of North Vietnam on the morning of October 26, 1966 a deadly fire broke out aboard the USS *Oriskany*, resulting in tragedy for the ship's air wing. It would be the first of two deadly fires aboard Navy aircraft carriers within the space of the year 1966/67 at the height of Operation Rolling Thunder.

Following the cancellation of a planned air strike because of bad weather over the target, the pilots and their planes stood down. Munitions were removed and returned to their armories. During this activity two young and inexperienced seamen accidently ignited one of the magnesium flares they were re-stowing. In their panic one threw the now-burning flare into a munitions storage locker that contained several hundred flares and a large number of 2.75-inch rockets. The resulting explosion created an intense fire that quickly spread into the nearby hangar bay. Men worked feverishly to remove planes and ordnance from the approaching inferno; more than 300 bombs were hauled out of the flames and jettisoned overboard. Other crewmen grabbed hoses and battled the blaze. Despite their initial success in averting disaster in the hangar bay, the fire and its thick, choking smoke was able to spread across four of the ship's levels. It quickly reached the officers' quarters where it trapped many unaware pilots in their staterooms.

It would be several hours before all the flames were extinguished, but thanks to the quick action of the crew and its damage control teams none of the ship's vital machinery was damaged. Unfortunately, rescue teams were not able to reach many of the trapped men in time: 36 officers, including 24 pilots of CVW-16, died of asphyxiation in their staterooms. Among the dead was the air wing's newly appointed CAG, Commander Rodney Carter. Eight enlisted men also died in the fire, bring the total loss of life to forty-four. In addition, 38 others were injured. Amazingly only three aircraft were destroyed, while three others suffered damage. After a brief stopover in the Philippines the *Oriskany* made her way back home for repairs, arriving in San Francisco on 16 November. Seven months later, a refurbished *Oriskany* would depart on her third, and most intense, deployment of the war.

Just nine months later and only five days into its initial on-line period, the USS *Forrestal* would become the victim of the Navy's worst operational accident of the war. When it was all over 134 men were dead and 62 were injured; 21 aircraft were destroyed or lost and another 43 damaged. The badly damaged ship would immediately depart Yankee Station for the United States and after nearly two years and $72 million in repairs, it would return to service for another 24 years. The *Forrestal*, however, would never make another Vietnam deployment.

It all began just before 11 a.m. on July 29, 1967 as the ship and its air wing were preparing to launch the second strike of the day. The *Forrestal's* flight deck was full of armed and fueled aircraft when an air-to-ground 5-inch Zuni rocket accidently fired from an F-4 Phantom. According to the Navy's investigation, the rocket then struck an A-4 Skyhawk belonging to VA-46, killing its pilot Lieutenant Commander Fred White, tearing apart the plane's external drop tank, and igniting a fire. One bomb that had been jarred loose from White's plane soon exploded, killing a number of firefighters and mortally wounding others. A river of burning jet fuel spread across the crowded flight deck, engulfing several nearby Skyhawks, including one piloted by Lieutenant Commander John McCain. McCain and his fellow pilots frantically

Mayhem on the *USS* Forrestal.

scrambled to escape the onrushing flames that quickly swallowed up their planes. Bombs and ammunition began to explode as they cooked off from the searing heat, creating massive holes in the flight deck and sending shrapnel skyward. Soon the entire fantail of the ship was engulfed in flames and rocked with more explosions. "It seemed as if the whole stern of the *Forrestal* had erupted," recalled one pilot.

Rushing to avert complete disaster, the deck crew bravely dove headlong into the flames to clear the deck of bombs and munitions before they detonated. Explosive ordnance specialists worked heroically to disarm smoldering bombs. Other crewmen worked to pull planes away from the oncoming flames or to jettison burning aircraft and debris over the side. Many died in the process. A number of sailors were blown overboard from the explosions and had to be rescued by helicopters or destroyers. Meanwhile, firefighting teams and volunteers battled to put out the flames. It was an uphill fight, but they made steady progress, joined in their efforts by two destroyers pumping water on the burning ship. Amazingly by 12.15 p.m. the fire on the flight deck fire was completely extinguished—some 75 minutes after it had started.

Despite this good news, the ship and its crew were far from safe. The four gaping holes in the flight deck allowed burning jet fuel to seep into the spaces below, triggering multiple secondary explosions, and spreading the flames across three levels below the flight deck. The fire also spread to one of the aft hangar bays. Moreover, the raging inferno and accompanying dense acrid smoke left large numbers of people cut off and trapped in various compartments below. In a race against time, damage control parties and volunteers fought desperately to contain the fires below and rescue their trapped fellow crewmen. Hampered by poor visibility, heavy smoke, and the intense heat, slow but steady progress was made. It would take the rest of the day and half the night before all the fires in the spaces below were completely extinguished. At 2 a.m. on July 30 all fires were reported out and the ship finally secured.

As the wounded *Forrestal* steamed westward toward home, Captain Beling praised his men in saying, "I am most proud of the way the crew reacted. The thing that is foremost in my mind is the concrete demonstration that I have seen of the worth of American youth."

Distractions and Disruptions

As Rolling Thunder appeared to be moving toward its climax at the start of 1968 with the outcome still in doubt, a number of unexpected developments far away from the skies over Hanoi and Haiphong began to take center stage. From the battlefields in South Vietnam to the Sea of Japan and the halls of power in Washington, a series of events in late 1967 and the early 1968 would ultimately seal the fate of the air campaign once and for all.

Although often overshadowed by high-profile alpha strikes in the northeast, the hundreds of daily armed recce missions across route packages I, II, and III in the southern panhandle were a central feature of the interdiction effort in the autumn of 1967. The Air

General Vo Nguyen Giap, responsible for implementing the North's military strategy in the South.

Force carried the burden of these daily missions, as well as larger strikes against the mountain passes into Laos and the important supply hub of Dong Hoi. The Navy, for its part, focused on transportation networks, lines of communication, and infrastructure around Vinh city and southward along the coast, while Marine aircraft operated against targets just north of the DMZ. Despite these efforts, U.S. intelligence estimated that in 1967 the flow of men, equipment, and supplies southward had been reduced by only 50 percent at best, a level that many believed was insignificant to affect the Viet Cong's and Hanoi's ability to prosecute the war in the South.[36] Moreover, General Vo Nguyen Giap had still been able to amass and supply a large force of men and heavy artillery that he used to regularly bombard and harass a line of U.S. Marine outposts just south of the DMZ all throughout the spring and summer.

Seeking to end this threat, General Westmoreland authorized Operation Neutralize in early September. The plan called for marshalling massive American firepower—artillery, naval gunfire, and air bombardment—to wipe out the North Vietnamese positions. Westmoreland granted General Momyer full centralized authority over all air assets engaged in the operation, much to consternation of Army and Marine commanders who wanted to maintain tactical control over their own aircraft. For 49 days the Americans attempted to root out the well-camouflaged and deeply dug-in enemy jungle positions just north of the DMZ by pounding them with artillery and bombs. When it was all over, American pilots had flown nearly 4,000 sorties, including 820 by B-52s in their first appearance over the North since the April 1966 bombing of Mu Gia Pass. An estimated 2,000 North Vietnamese soldiers were killed and their guns silenced.[37] The Marine outposts were secure, at least for now. Although successful in eliminating the immediate threat to U.S. forces in South Vietnam, Operation Neutralize diverted Air Force and Navy assets away from Rolling Thunder missions at a critical time when Admiral Sharp needed them to maintain the maximum pressure on Hanoi and Haiphong.

Just prior to the start of 1968 electronic monitoring along DMZ and in southern Laos indicated a flurry of activity along the Ho Chi Minh Trail and it was soon confirmed by U.S. intelligence that a large buildup was in progress.[38] In early January, Marines at the westernmost outpost south of the DMZ at Khe Sanh, only about five miles from the Laotian border, confirmed the presence of large numbers of North Vietnamese troops. Soon the base was surrounded by an estimated 20,000 men from three regular North Vietnamese divisions, who were equipped with long-range howitzers, anti-aircraft artillery, and even PT-76 light tanks. Despite growing concern in some circles—including within the White House—that Khe Sanh was another Dien Bein Phu in the making, Westmoreland choose to reinforce the garrison to bring its strength up to 6,000 men. Unlike the French situation in 1954, the Americans held an overwhelming artillery advantage in and around their base and could call on a vast reserve of air power, so Westmoreland remained confident in his ability to blunt any enemy attack.[39]

This confidence would be tested soon enough. The battle began on January 21, 1968 with a sapper attack on one of Khe Sanh's external positions, which was then followed by an intense artillery barrage against the main base. The siege was on and the garrison cut off, now completely dependent on air resupply for its survival. Flying into the base forced pilots to run a gauntlet of enemy fire and conduct touch-and-go landings, discharging cargo and troops from still-moving planes. As challenging as the resupply effort was, General Momyer viewed the large North Vietnamese troop concentrations around Khe Sanh as a golden opportunity to unleash the full fury of American air power. As the air commander for Operation Niagara (the codename for the defense of

B-52 heavy bombers played a relatively minor role in Rolling Thunder, instead focusing on interdiction efforts in Laos and providing battlefield support in South Vietnam. (Photo National Museum of the U.S. Air Force)

Khe Sanh), Momyer was able to call on all available aircraft in South Vietnam, as well as those in Thailand and from TF-77. An average day would see 350 tactical fighter strikes, 60 B-52 bombing sorties, and dozens of airborne forward air control aircraft directing artillery fire. "We never let up," said Momyer.[40] Ground stations guided radar bombing missions during bad weather and also allowed B-52s to drop their devastating payloads within three-quarters of a mile of the camp's perimeter. "The tonnage of ordnance that has been placed in a five-mile circle around [the base] is unbelievable," said one commander. "It is just a landscape of splinters and bomb craters."[41]

Toward the end of March, General Giap began withdrawing his forces. On April 1 elements of the Army's 1st Cavalry Division began clearing the road westward to the base, finally linking up with the Marines on the 6th. The 77-day siege was over. North Vietnamese casualties were estimated at between 10,000 and 15,000 against the loss of 205 Americans.[42] U.S. planes had dropped in excess of 100,000 tons of ordnance and delivered 12,400 tons of supplies while flying nearly 25,000 sorties, at the cost of six aircraft (three of which were transports) destroyed.[43]

The opening round of the battle of Khe Sanh, however, was quickly overshadowed by a much larger countrywide threat on January 31—the Tet Offensive. Although an offensive around the Vietnamese holiday and truce had been anticipated by Westmoreland and his generals, the sheer scope and audacity of the attack stunned the

Americans. Some 70,000–100,000 Viet Cong guerrillas and North Vietnamese regulars attempted to capture all 36 South Vietnamese provincial capitals, as well as Saigon and provoke a popular uprising. These attacks were accompanied by several high-profile sapper assaults on symbols of American power, including the U.S. Embassy in Saigon and the main airbases at Bien Hoa, Tan San Nhut, and Da Nang. Following the initial chaos, American and South Vietnamese troops with extensive air support began to systematically expel the attackers in the coming weeks from the towns and cities they had captured. However, the fighting in the imperial city of Hue in the northern part of the country—where the Viet Cong flag fluttered defiantly over the ancient citadel— lasted through most of February. It left the city in ruins with as many as 10,000 civilian dead and more than 80 percent of population homeless, before it was retaken.[44] The last of the resistance was quelled by the beginning of March, leaving more than 40,000 communist fighters dead, while the combined American and South Vietnamese losses totaled 3,400.[45]

Well-hidden supply and ammunition depots were difficult to spot and destroy; "sometimes it felt like we were just bombing the jungle." (Photo National Museum of the U.S. Air Force)

Neither the Americans nor their South Vietnamese allies were prepared for the scale and ferocity of the Tet Offensive in January / February 1968.

The abject failure of the Tet Offensive and the heavy losses sustained during the siege of Khe Sanh were a devastating military setback for Hanoi. While the Americans and the South Vietnamese were victorious on the battlefield, the timing and psychological impact of these events could not have been worse for the Johnson administration. The White House and hawks in the administration and Congress had spent much of the past six months trying to convince their opponents and, moreover, the American public that victory in Vietnam was in hand. There was light at the end of the tunnel. The images of a battle-scarred embassy with the bodies of Viet Cong dead, hulks of burnt-out American planes at Bien Hoa and Da Nang, and smoke rising from the rubble of Vietnamese cities, however, was difficult for many Americans to reconcile with Westmoreland proclamation of a convincing American victory. Hanoi may have been beaten on the battlefield in South Vietnam, but it was on the verge of winning on the streets of the United States after Tet.

A week prior to the momentous events of Tet, Washington was facing a more immediate crisis and even the prospect of another war in Asia. On January 23, North Korean naval craft fired on and then seized the American intelligence-gathering ship, the USS *Pueblo*, while it was operating in the Sea of Japan in international waters. Pyongyang claimed the attack, which left one American dead and four wounded, was in response to U.S. provocations and a violation of its territorial waters. The seized ship was brought to the port of Wonsan and its 83-man crew then subject to intense and brutal torture in an effort to extract "a confession." In response, President Johnson ordered 350 planes and the deployment of a 25-warship task force led by the USS *Enterprise* (detached from Rolling Thunder operations) to the Korean peninsula, along with a call-up of 14,000 Air Force and Navy reservists.[46] Diplomatic efforts eventually led to the release of the crew eleven months later, but the *Pueblo* incident remained an ongoing distraction throughout 1968.

Admiral Sharp sought to use the shock of Tet to finally persuade Johnson to unleash the full weight of American power against "the source of aggression—the enemy's heartland, the Hanoi/Haiphong center of North Vietnamese power."[47] In this he had the full support of the General Wheeler and the other Joint Chiefs, who recommended bombing targets in the Chinese buffer zone, vastly reducing the size of the prohibited zones around Hanoi and Haiphong, and closing Haiphong's harbor through a combination of air attacks and mining.[48] Not only would these actions provide a strong and immediate military response, but they would signal American political resolve. Although sound military reasoning, U.S. commanders were out of touch with the extent and degree of the growing anti-war sentiment in the United States and unaware of just how much the psychological wound of Tet had turned the tide in favor of de-escalation. They were about to find out soon.

The Tet Aftermath: The Air Campaign Winds Down

Despite the loss of credibility to the administration as a result of Tet, President Johnson and many of his key advisers still believed that the United States would prevail in the long run. Nonetheless, the doves within the administration were steadily building a case for American de-escalation and eventual disengagement from Vietnam. They highlighted the failure of Westmoreland's troop buildup to check, let alone eradicate the communist insurgency. They pointed to the ineffectiveness of nearly three years of bombing to interdict the flow of men and matériel southward or to compel Hanoi to negotiate. On this latter issue it was said that all the air campaign had shown was that "a relatively underdeveloped Asian country with a surplus of men can stand an awful lot of bombing with saying 'uncle.'"[49] Moreover, according to Deputy Secretary of Defense Paul Nitze's critique, the United States was spending billions of dollars and incurring heavy losses of men and planes for very marginal results and as long as the flow of supplies from China and the Soviet Union continued it would be impossible to disrupt the war-making capacity of the North Vietnamese.[50]

In early March 1968, after an extensive review and discussion with senior military commanders and his civilian deputies, newly appointed Secretary of Defense Clark Clifford sided with those calling for de-escalation by noting that "the military course we are pursuing was not only hopeless but endless."[51] Johnson's Vietnam policy was also under increasing attack by his political opponents. On March 12 Senator William Fulbright, a leading critic of the war, used hearings on military assistance to the Saigon government as a public forum to debate U.S. policy in Vietnam. Even more telling on that same day, the President narrowly defeated Senator Eugene McCarthy—another staunch critic—in the New Hampshire presidential primary. Four days later Robert Kennedy declared his candidacy for the Democratic Party nomination. The walls were closing in on Johnson.

Nonetheless, the White House continued to try to rally public support by warning of the catastrophic consequences of failure. The final straw came in late March when a highly respected group of the President's informal senior advisers told him that there was likely no realistic chance of military victory and any escalation of the war and the bombing would be pointless.[52] Johnson thus reluctantly agreed to halt the bombing north of 20th parallel and decided against Westmoreland's troop request. Then on March 31 after publicly informing the nation of these decisions to de-escalate the war, Johnson announced that he would not seek re-election. A few days later, Hanoi agreed to enter into preliminary talks with United States in Paris.

This was the beginning of the end for Rolling Thunder, although it would take some time for the air campaign to wind down completely. In fact the first three months of the year saw a continuation of bombing efforts to maintain the pressure on Hanoi and Haiphong with the transportation and logistics network under repeated attack as were

The entry of the A-7 Corsair II with its advanced avionics and technology into the air campaign at the end of 1967 provided the Navy with another effective tool, but it proved too late for Rolling Thunder. (Photo Emil Buehler Library, National Naval Aviation Museum)

the major airfields at Hoa Loa, Kep, Phu Yen, and Yen Bai. While there were fewer alpha strikes, commanders made the most of their opportunities with the all-weather A-6s playing a vital role in night missions. They would also pay a high price: eight Navy and Marine Intruders were lost in the first quarter of 1968, four of which were flown by VA-35.[53] One major target that did warrant a concerted effort was an old nemesis—the Thanh Hoa bridge. On the early morning of January 28, 44 Air Force and Navy aircraft rained down 140 tons of bombs on the bridge over the course of three and half hours. The attack heavily damaged the bridge's metal superstructure, left the southern rail line twisted and torn asunder, and the southern approaches extensively cratered beyond recognition.[54] But the bridge still remained standing. Although the Americans suffered no losses, they knew that they would be forced one day to return to the Dragon's Jaw. No one ever thought that the day would lie more than four years in the future.

The poor operating conditions in the northeast pushed a lot of air activity farther south along the coast and the outbreak of the Tet Offensive diverted assets into South Vietnam for close air support missions. Noteworthy in this latter respect were the final combat sorties of the war for the Navy's A-1 Skyraider; VA-25 would fly the final mission against enemy artillery around Khe Sanh on February 20.[55] The military and logistics hubs at Vinh and Dong Hoi continued to receive special attention as did the supply routes to the far south and across the western mountain passes into Laos.

More disturbing for the Americans was the continuing success of the VPAF, which in the first quarter of 1968 accounted for an astonishing 22 percent of American losses.[56] During this time the American would lose nine aircraft to MiGs, while shooting down five MiG-17s and four MiG-21s—a disturbing 1:1 loss ratio. The VPAF scored a major psychological victory on January 14 when one of its MiG-21s downed an EB-66 electronic countermeasures plane for the first time with an Atoll missile. Hit directly in its starboard engine while orbiting at 29,000 feet west of Thanh Hoa, the mortally wounded plane nearly reached the Laotian border before the seven-man crew was forced to bail out. Multiple rescue attempts were made over the next three days that resulted in the loss of one Air Force helicopter and saw two others seriously damaged by small-arms fire, but three crewmen were recovered. The remaining four, however, were captured by local militia.[57] A few days later, MiG-17s jumped a flight of F-4s from the 435th TFS out of Ubon that was attacking the Bac Giang power plant northeast of Hanoi. Following a prolonged dogfight two Phantoms and one MiG were shot down.[58]

The ceremonial welcoming back after completing 100 missions; note the scarf with the names of previous centennial members. (Photo National Museum of the U.S. Air Force)

Another milestone was achieved by the VPAF on February 3 when MiG-21s engaged a pair of F-102 Delta Daggers flying combat air patrol just inside the North Vietnamese–Laotian border. The ensuing engagement saw an exchange of air-to-air missiles with the MiGs drawing first blood and fatally damaged one of the F-102s, which eventually crashed into the jungle killing the pilot.[59] The Americans responded by redoubling their strikes against enemy airfields, but extremely poor weather, as well as the ability of the VPAF to operate safely from Hanoi's Gia Lam airfield and bases in southern China greatly hindered the effort.

Things were not standing still for the Americans as they sought ways to improve their tactical and operational bombing effectiveness. Seasonal weather problems were constantly forcing the cancellation of large numbers of missions, because of the lack of target visibility. While the Navy overcame this problem somewhat with the introduction of the A-6 and steadily evolving avionics for its fleet of attack aircraft, the Air Force struggled to find an acceptable solution. Radar bombing often provided mixed results and left the strike force, flying a fixed heading and altitude, highly vulnerable to missiles and anti-aircraft fire. The introduction of long-range navigation radio aids (LORAN) in March allowed bombing at higher altitudes, but the system had limited coverage and lacked the accuracy needed for pinpoint bombing. Thus, it was with much fanfare that a detachment of advanced F-111 aircraft arrived in Takhli, Thailand under the code name Combat Lancer in mid-March 1968. With its high-speed, long-range, heavy payload capacity, and advanced terrain-following and radar bombing technology the plane was a potential game changer.[60] However, there were problems from the outset that seemed to confirm the belief that the new aircraft had been rushed too quickly into combat. The first F-111 was lost over Route Pack I just north of the DMZ under mysterious circumstances on the night of March 28. A few days later another encountered control problems, forcing the crew to eject over Thai airspace. The final straw came on April 22 during a Steel Tiger mission over southern Laos when it appears the aircraft flew into the ground during a low-level attack. All further combat missions were suspended, although local training flights in Thailand continued. The four remaining planes were eventually withdrawn in November after flying only 55 combat sorties.[61]

The first half of the year would also see the introduction of several new technologies, including a new anti-radiation missile and the nascent development of laser-guided bombs. The Standard ARM or what would become the AGM-78 had a larger warhead that its predecessor, the AGM-45 Shrike, and had the capability to lock on to enemy acquisition radars from a much greater distance.[62] It was soon in use by April for Air Force and Navy Iron Hand flights, although Shrikes would still continue to be used. The first generation of bombs fitted with steerable fins and laser homing devices was introduced in May and held the promise of more precision delivery and the use of fewer bombs.[63]

While all these developments boded well for the increased future effectiveness of American air power, they came too late for Rolling Thunder. President Johnson's peace negotiation gambit at the end of March with his suspension of U.S. bombing north of the 20th parallel (and its later extension southward to the 19th parallel by April 5) brought the strategic coercive element of the air campaign to an end once and for all. The bombing of the North would still continue for the next seven months, but only in the southern panhandle of route packages I, II, and the lower half of III. Moreover, the air campaign now evolved into a pure interdiction operation striking lines of communication and supply as a part of the extended battlefield in South Vietnam, despite the marginal success in the past. A few larger strikes were flown too, but worthwhile targets were few and far between in this heavily bombed part of the North.

Psychologically the waning months of 1968 were difficult for the American pilots. They often found themselves forced to seek out isolated groups of vehicles, barges, and small boats or were relegated to bombing hillside cave storage areas and suspect jungle crossroads, which was a far cry from the adrenaline rush of flying alpha strikes against major bridges around Hanoi or Haiphong. While the threat environment in the southern panhandle was more forgiving than up north, the North Vietnamese defenders continued to take their toll of American aircraft. Both the Vinh and Dong Hoi areas were especially well protected and teeming with hundreds of 37-mm, 57-mm, and

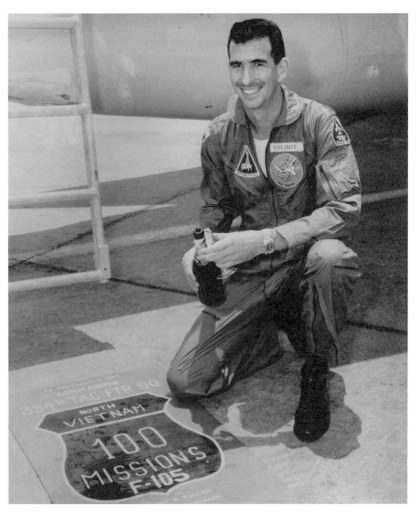

Completing 100 missions was a major milestone for any Air Force pilot or crew member. (Photo National Museum of the U.S. Air Force)

85-mm anti-aircraft guns, as well as the occasional SA-2 battery. Of the 65 U.S. combat losses from April to the end of October, 35 percent were in the Dong Hoi area and 41 percent were in the Vinh city area.[64]

The VPAF also maintained its aggressive posture with mixed results. An ill-advised attempt to stage two MiG-17 fighters from the 923rd Regiment out of Vinh airfield in mid-June ended in disaster with the destruction of both aircraft by an American air strike within minutes of their arrival.[65] Relying on hit and run tactics to ambush U.S. planes before fleeing back to safety north of the 19th parallel showed more promise with the downing of two Navy Phantoms in May and June by MiG-21s.[66] The 923rd Regiment's MiG-17s also claimed to have destroyed three other enemy aircraft in July, but no American losses were recorded.[67] Meanwhile, during the summer months, Navy F-4s and F-8s shot down three MiG-21s and two MiG-17s.[68] Lieutenant Anthony Nargi of VF-111, flying his Crusader off the deck of the USS *Intrepid*, tallied the final air victory of the year on September 19 when he and his wingman intercepted a flight of MiG-21s seeking to disrupt an A-4 strike north of Vinh. In the ensuing engagement Nargi was able to destroy one of the MiG-21s with an AIM-9 Sidewinder missile, the last official air-to-air victory for the F-8 of the Vietnam War and of Rolling Thunder.[69]

Then it was all over. President Johnson, increasingly hopeful that the North Vietnamese would now join the United States in de-escalating the war and moving toward a peaceful resolution, ordered an end to all bombing of the North, effective November 1, 1968. Just prior to Johnson's announcement, Major Frank Lenahan of the 8th TFW carried out the last bombing mission of Rolling Thunder on October 31 when he attacked a target near Dong Hoi in his F-4 and returned safely to Thailand. After more than three and half years the air campaign had come to an end.

Mk-82 and -83 bombs. (Photo USAF Museum)

7. POST-MORTEM

With President Johnson's ceasing all air strikes on North Vietnam, Operation Rolling Thunder—the largest sustained American bombing campaign ever conducted—came to an inglorious end. After three years and eight months, American pilots and their South Vietnamese allies had flown almost 300,000 sorties and delivered more than 600,000 tons of bombs.[1] Their targets ranged from critical transportation, economic, and industrial infrastructure to all types of military installations in an effort to bring about a negotiated settlement to the communist insurgency in the South. The effort would cost the lives of 671 American pilots and crews, more than 900 U.S. aircraft of all types, and the expenditure of billions of dollars.[2] The air campaign was estimated to have inflicted in excess of $425 million in damage to the North Vietnamese economy, destroyed 85 percent of the North's major industrial capacity, and forced Hanoi to divert up to 500,000 people to maintain the functioning of its transportation and supply network.[3] But, in the end, the United States was neither able to break the political will of the North Vietnamese or destroy their capacity to continue the war.

The Johnson administration's failure to accomplish its central objective of bringing the war to an early close and disengaging the United States was certainly not for lack of trying. Nor was it, because the United States put too much reliance on military might— via air power in this instance—to achieve its goal. Instead, Rolling Thunder was at its core a strategic failure in the most fundamental sense given the inability of American civilian and military leadership to agree on how to effectively align ends, ways, and means into a coherent war strategy. Instead, clashing and often conflicting strategies evolved over the course of the air campaign that were the result of compromise and expediency. That this approach, which included highly restrictive rules of engagement, White House micromanagement of target selection, and repeated bombing pauses, satisfied no one and was recognized as deeply flawed, comes as little surprise. Nevertheless, these concerns were swept under the rug in the desire to do something and maintain the momentum of the bombing effort once it had begun.

Thus, what started out as a tool of coercive diplomacy, intended to pressure Hanoi and signal American resolve became a mish-mash of disjointed political and military policies in search of a common strategy. While Ambassador Maxwell Taylor cautioned on the one hand that the targets being attacked were less important than the message being sent, American military commanders on the other hand saw an opportunity to at least cripple, if not destroy much of the North's war-making capability and hinder its ability to support the Viet Cong insurgency. The history of Rolling Thunder clearly reflects this dynamic. Initially used as a mechanism to apply gradually increasing pressure on Hanoi to gain political concessions, the bombing then morphed into an interdiction effort to limit Viet Cong advances in the South before transforming itself into a strategic bombing effort (limited though it was) to quash the North's ability and will to prosecute the war. After April 1968 it returned to an interdiction effort south of the 19th parallel once again.

Not surprisingly, military–civilian tensions, as well as internal Johnson administration divisions, were palatable as various factions sought to mold Rolling Thunder to fit their

It's over. President Johnson scans a newspaper announcing the end of all bombing of North Vietnam, November 1, 1968. (Photo LBJ Library)

own vision. None was successful. What emerged then was a campaign built around compromise and a lack of strategic direction, one that was continually in flux and driven by the hope that American firepower and persistence would ultimately overcome these deficiencies. This proved to be its undoing.

There has been much speculation over the years as to whether the air campaign could have—had it been conducted differently—been a decisive factor in shorting the war by several years and saving tens of thousands of American and Vietnamese lives. Although this belief taps into the popular narrative as to the bungling and mishandling of the war by the Johnson administration and McNamara along with his civilian number crunchers at the Pentagon in particular, it is probably just wishful thinking. Could the bombing campaign have been more effective? Absolutely. As it has been noted throughout the previous chapters there were a significant number of tactical, operational, and strategic mistakes and misjudgments made during the course of Rolling Thunder. This happens in any war. In the end, it failed for the simple reason that Ho Chi Minh and the communist leadership were neither ready nor willing to negotiate an end to the war in 1965—or in 1966, 1967 or 1968 for that matter. They knew how to play the "long war;" one of psychological and physical attrition that the Vietnamese had used to outlast various conquerors or would-be conquerors from the Chinese to the Japanese to the French. Ho Chi Minh could afford to wait out the Americans, but Johnson could not afford to wait out the North Vietnamese. It was a hard and costly lesson for the Americans to learn.

Yet the Americans did learn from the failure of Rolling Thunder and when they had another opportunity in 1972, things were done differently. This time overwhelming air power was unleashed against the North. Under Operations Linebacker I & II, North Vietnamese ports were closed by mining and critical targets in the North's heartland were subject to unrelenting attack. Moreover, faced with the very real prospect of jeopardizing the American withdrawal it had sought so long to achieve, Hanoi finalized the 1973 Paris Peace Accords ending U.S. military involvement in Vietnam. For the American pilots and personnel the results were bittersweet. They accomplished much and proved themselves over and over again. Yet they remained frustrated and complained about how those back in Washington were out of touch with the reality of the air war and they knew they could accomplish so much more. Nonetheless, they were professionals to the end and day after day they flew the missions they were given, fighting the war they had, rather than the one they wanted to fight. And that was their lasting legacy.

"I never met him." (Photo Ed Schipul)

NOTES

Chapter 1: A Place Called Vietnam

1. F. Logevall, *Embers of War*, p. 624.
2. *The Pentagon Papers*, "U.S. and France in Indochina, 1950–56," pp. 179-215.
3. E. Doyle, et. al, *Passing the Torch*, p. 136.
4. Ibid.
5. Ibid., p. 106.
6. Logevall, p. 689.
7. S. Karnow, *Vietnam,* p. 229.
8. Logevall, p. 697.
9. P. Mersky, *F-8 Crusader Units*, pp. 16-17.
10. P. Paterson, "The Truth about Tonkin," *Naval History Magazine.*
11. J. and S. Stockdale, *In Love and War*, p. 23 as cited in Paterson.
12. L. Johnson, "Report on the Gulf of Tonkin Incident (August 4, 1964)."
13. Mersky, *F-8 Crusader Units*, p. 19.
14. U.S. Sharp, *Strategy for Defeat*, p. 44.
15. T. Maitland and S. Weiss, *Raising the Stakes*, p. 160.
16. Gulf of Tonkin Resolution (1964).

Chapter 2: A Gathering Storm

1. J. Morrocco, *Thunder From Above*, p. 30.
2. *Pentagon Papers*, "U.S. Programs in South Vietnam, NOV 1963-APR 1965," p. 47.
3. Ibid, p. ii.
4. Ibid.
5. Sharp, p. 52.
6. C. LeMay, *Mission with LeMay*, p. 565.
7. *Pentagon Papers*, "Military Pressures Against North Vietnam, NOV–DEC 1964," p. iii.
8. Sharp, p. 58.
9. *Pentagon Papers*, "Military Pressures Against North Vietnam, NOV–DEC 1964," p. 8.
10. Ibid., p. i.
11. Ibid, p. v.
12. Morrocco, p. 31.
13. Maitland and Weiss, *Raising the Stakes*, p. 165.
14. Sharp, p. 56.
15. J. Van Staaveren, *Gradual Failure*, p. 9.
16. Morrocco, p. 34.
17. Van Staaveren, p. 15.
18. Ibid, p. 17.
19. Morrocco, p. 36-37; Van Staaveren, p. 18.
20. Morrocco, p. 37; Van Staaveren, p. 24.
21. Morrocco, pp. 37-39.
22. Sharp, p. 60.
23. Morrocco, p. 40; Van Staaveren, p. 25.

24. J. Correll, "Rolling Thunder," p. 60.

25. "CINCPAC message to JCS," 17 February 1965 as quoted in Sharp, pp. 61-62.

Chapter 3: The Air Campaign Unfolds

1. J. Morrocco, *Thunder From Above*, pp. 52-53.
2. Ibid., p. 53.
3. Ibid.
4. J. Van Staaveren, *Gradual Failure*, pp. 85-86.
5. Ibid., p. 86.
6. *The Pentagon Papers*, "The Air War in North Vietnam: Rolling Thunder Begins," pp. 333-334.
7. Ibid., pp. 334.
8. Ibid., pp. 336.
9. Ibid., p. 337.
10. Sharp, *Strategy for Defeat*, p. 67.
11. Ibid, p. 69.
12. Gus Gudmunson interview, March 2016.
13. A. Lavalle, "The Tale of Two Bridges," p. 9.
14. OSD/NPIC Imagery Report J-6976, "Bridge Interdiction North Vietnam," April 11, 1965.
15. Lavalle, p. 36.
16. W. Boyne, "Breaking the Dragon's Jaw," p. 59.
17. Ibid.
18. C. Hobson, *Vietnam Air Losses*, p. 17.
19. Van Staaveren, p. 108.
20. Morrocco, p. 60.
21. Ibid., p. 61.
22. Van Staaveren, p. 96.
23. N. Polmar and E. Marolda, *Naval Air War: The Rolling Thunder Campaign*, p. 3.
24. Morrocco, p. 56.
25. K. Goodwin, *Lyndon Johnson and the American Dream*, pp. 264-265.
26. Morrocco, p. 64.
27. Sharp, p. 80.

Chapter 4: A Building Whirlwind

1. J. Van Staaveren, *Gradual Failure*, p. 137.
2. U.S. Sharp, *Strategy for Defeat*, p. 85.
3. Van Staaveren, p. 138.
4. P. Davies, *F-105 Thunderchief Units*, p. 28
5. Data drived from "The Contemporary Historical Examination of Current Operations Reports of Southeast Asia, 1961-1975" as cited by R. Frankum, *Like Rolling Thunder*, p. 30.
6. Van Staaveren, p. 140.
7. C. Hobson, *Vietnam Air Losses*, pp. 21-27.
8. Data derived from "The Contemporary Historical Examination of Current Operations Reports of Southeast Asia, 1961-1975" as cited by Frankum, p. 30.
9. Davies, p. 28; Van Staaveren, p. 151.
10. W. Westmoreland, *A Soldier Reports*, p. 142-143; L. Johnson, *Vantage Point*, p. 146.
11. Van Staaveren, p. 155.

12. Ibid., 141.
13. Ibid.
14. J. Nichols and B. Tillman, *On Yankee Station*, p. 50.
15. Imagery report, CSD/NPIC 214/65, "Railway and Highway Bridge, Thanh Hoa, North Vietnam, 1950N 10548E," 29 April 1965.
16. Frankum, p. 29.
17. Van Staaveren, pp. 158-159.
18. Westmoreland, pp. 144-145.
19. J. Smith, *Rolling Thunder*, p. 68
20. Nichols and Tillman, p. 56.
21. Ibid.
22. Ibid., p. 55.
23. Ibid., p. 58.
24. Hobson, p. 26.
25. Ibid., p. 29.
26. Ibid.
27. J. Morrocco, *Thunder From Above*, p. 111.
28. Hobson, pp. 43-44.
29. Nichols and Tillman, p. 60.
30. Van Staaveren, pp. 147-148.
31. Ibid., p. 210.
32. U.S. Naval Institute, *Naval History Magazine*, "Carrier Air and Vietnam," April 1987.
33. Nichols and Tillman, p. 104.
34. Van Staaveren, p. 209.
35. Ibid., p. 192.
36. Hobson, pp. 34-35.
37. Van Staaveren, p. 201.
38. Ibid., p. 203.
39. Ibid., p. 204.
40. Hobson, p. 44.
41. Van Staaveren, p. 213.

Chapter 5: Fury from Above

1. J. Van Staaveren, *Gradual Failure*, p. 215.
2. CIA, *President's Daily Brief*, January 13, 1966.
3. U.S. Sharp, *Strategy for Defeat*, p. 109.
4. Ibid., p. 110.
5. Ibid, p. 111.
6. Van Staaveren, p. 225.
7. Ibid., p. 226.
8. Ibid., p. 268.
9. C. Hobson, *Vietnam Air Losses*, p. 49.
10. Ibid., pp. 50-53.
11. Ibid., pp. 48-55.
12. Van Staaveren, p. 270.
13. J. Smith, *Rolling Thunder*, p. 89.

14. Hobson, p. 57.
15. P. Davies, *F-105 Thunderchief Units*, p. 36.
16. Hobson, pp. 55-60.
17. W. Westmoreland, *A Soldier Reports*, p. 234.
18. Van Staaveren, p. 252-253.
19. Smith, pp. 89-90.
20. Van Staaveren, p. 253.
21. Ibid., p. 251.
22. Ibid., p. 280.
23. Ibid.
24. Ibid, p. 290.
25. Ibid, pp. 292-293.
26. J. Morrocco, *Thunder From Above*, p. 128.
27. Ibid, p. 130.
28. J. Levinson, *Alpha Strike Vietnam*, pp. 139-141.
29. Hobson, pp. 69-70.
30. Morrocco, p. 131.
31. Smith, p. 339.
32. Ibid., p. 102.
33. Morrocco, p. 143.
34. Smith, pp. 342-343; Hobson, p. 271.
35. Hobson, pp. 82-84.
36. Smith, p. 114.
37. Ibid.
38. R. Frankum, *Like Rolling Thunder*, p. 54.
39. Ibid.
40. Morrocco, p. 144.
41. Hobson, pp. 85-90 and 270.
42. Smith, p. 120.
43. Ibid.
44. Hobson, pp. 85-90.
45. Smith, p. 122.
46. Davies, p. 46.
47. Morrocco, p. 150.
48. Hobson, p. 91.
49. Morrocco, p. 150.
50. A. Lavalle, "A Tale of Two Bridges," pp. 57-58.
51. Ibid., p. 58.
52. Morrocco, p. 149.
53. *New York Times*, April 21, 1967.
54. Davies, F-105s, p. 48.
55. Hobson, p. 96.
56. A-4s, pp. 42-43.
57. Hobson, p. 98.
58. Hobson, pp. 93-100.
59. Davies, pp. 74-75.

60. Smith, p. 341.
61. Hobson, p. 102. Sadly, Commander Smith would not live to see this success. He was shot down the previous day while attacking the Bac Giang power plant northwest of Hanoi, taken prisoner, and then died within a few days after being tortured.
62. Hobson, pp. 101-102.
63. Hobson, p. 102.
64. C. Berger, *The United States Air Force in Southeast Asia*, 83.
65. Smith, pp. 340-342.
66. R. McNamara, *In Retrospect*, pp. 286-290.
67. Ibid., p. 269.
68. Ibid., p. 313.
69. Morrocco, p. 154.
70. Sharp, pp. 179-180.
71. Morrocco, p. 154.
72. L. Johnson, *Vantage Point*, p. 240.
73. McNamara, p. 290.

Chapter 6: Once More into the Breach

1. U.S. Sharp, *Strategy for Defeat*, p. 180.
2. Ibid., p. 181.
3. Ibid., 180 and 185.
4. Ibid., p. 159.
5. C. Hobson, *Vietnam Air Losses*, p. 107.
6. Ibid., p. 109.
7. R. Francillon, *Tonkin Gulf Yacht Club*, pp. 152-154.
8. J. Morrocco, *Thunder From Above*, p. 157.
9. Ibid.
10. J. Frisbee, "A Place Called the Doumer Bridge," p. 100; P. Davies, *F-105 Thunderchief Units*, pp. 50-51.
11. J. Levinson, *Alpha Strike*, p. 208.
12. Ibid, pp. 207-209; P. Mersky, *A-4 Skyhawk Units*, p. 51.
13. Levinson, p. 207.
14. Mersky, *A-4 Skyhawk Units*, p. 51.
15. Hobson, p. 114.
16. Ibid.
17. J. Smith, *Rolling Thunder*, p. 342.
18. Morrocco, p. 158.
19. Hobson, p. 116.
20. Morrocco, p. 157.
21. Ibid., pp. 157-158.
22. Smith, pp. 144-145.
23. Ibid., p. 145.
24. Hobson, p. 122.
25. Davies, p. 51.
26. Hobson, p. 123.
27. Ibid.
28. I. Toperczer, *MiG-17 and MiG-19 Units*, pp. 48-49.

29. Hobson, pp. 126-127.
30. Ibid., p. 128.
31. Toperczer, p. 49.
32. Davies, p. 79; Smith, p. 343.
33. N. Birzer and P. Mersky. *A-7 Corsair II Units*, p. 26.
34. Smith, p. 148.
35. Morrocco, p. 183.
36. R. McNamara, *In Retrospect*, pp. 275, 286 287; Joint Chiefs, "War in Vietnam, Part 3," p. 85.
37. Morrocco, p. 176.
38. Morrocco, p. 178; Westmoreland, *A Soldier Reports*, p. 316.
39. Westmoreland, pp. 335-339.
40. Morrocco, p. 178.
41. Ibid. p. 179.
42. Westmoreland, p. 347.
43. Westmoreland, p. 340; Hobson, pp. 134-144; Morrocco, p. 181.
44. J. Olson, *In Country*, p. 264-265.
45. Ibid.
46. J. Cheevers, "The Pueblo Scapegoat."
47. Sharp, pp. 215-216.
48. Morrocco, p. 182
49. Ibid., p. 183.
50. Ibid.
51. Ibid.
52. Ibid., p. 183-184.
53. Hobson, pp. 134-143.
54. A. Lavalle, "Tale of Two Bridges," p. 63.
55. R. Burgess and R. Rausa, *A-1 Skyraider Units*, p. 86.
56. Morrocco, p. 159.
57. Hobson, p. 135.
58. Hobson, p. 133; Smith, p. 343.
59. Hobson, p. 135.
60. Ibid., p. 143.
61. Ibid., p. 146.
62. Smith, p. 160.
63. Ibid, p. 164.
64. Hobson, pp. 144-166.
65. Toperczer, p. 51.
66. Hobson, p. 271.
67. Toperczer, p. 52.
68. Smith, p. 343.
69. P. Mersky, *F-8 Crusader Units*, p. 55; Smith, p. 344.

Chapter 7: Post-Mortem

1. Smith, *Rolling Thunder*, p. 166.
2. Ibid.
3. CIA and DIA, "An Appraisal of the Bombing of North Vietnam."

BIBLIOGRAPHY

Berger, Carl (ed.). *The United States Air Force in Southeast Asia, 1961–1973*. Washington, DC: Office of Air Force History, U.S. Air Force, 1984.

Burgess, Richard and Rosario Rausa. *U.S. Navy A-1 Skyraider Units of the Vietnam War*. Oxford, UK: Osprey Publishing, 2009.

Birzer, Norman and Peter Mersky. *U.S. Navy A-7 Corsair II Units of the Vietnam War*. Oxford, UK: Osprey Publishing, 2004.

Boyne, Walter. "Breaking the Dragon's Jaw," *Air Force Magazine*, August 2011.

Campbell, Douglas. *U.S. Navy and U.S. Marine Corps Aircraft Damaged or Destroyed During the Vietnam War. Volume 1: Listed by Ship Attached and by Squadron*. Syneca Research Group, 2015.

Central Intelligence Agency. *President's Daily Brief*. Washington, DC: January 13, 1966.

_____ and Defense Intelligence Agency. "An Appraisal of the Bombing of North Vietnam through 31 January 1968." Secret, undated.

Cheevers, Jack. "The Pueblo Scapegoat." *Naval History Magazine*, Vol. 28, No. 5, October 2014.

Correll, John. "Rolling Thunder," *Air Force Magazine*. March 2005: 58-65.

Cosmas, Graham. "The Joint Chiefs of Staff and The War in Vietnam, 1960–1968, Part 3." Washington, DC: Office of Joint History, Office of the Chairman of the Joint Chiefs of Staff, 2009.

Davies, Peter. *F-105 Thunderchief Units of the Vietnam War*. Oxford, UK: Osprey Publishing, 2010.

_____. *USAF F-4 Phantom II MiG Killers 1965-68*. Oxford, UK: Osprey Publishing, 2004.

Doyle, Edward, Samuel Lipsman and Stephen Weiss (eds). *The Vietnam Experience: Passing the Torch*. Boston: Boston Publishing Company, 1981.

Francillon, René. *Tonkin Gulf Yacht Club: U.S. Carrier Operations off Vietnam*. London: Conway Maritime Press Ltd, 1988. Naval Institute Press edition, Annapolis, MD.

Frankum, Ronald. *Like Rolling Thunder: The Air War in Vietnam, 1964–1975*. Lanham, MD: Rowman & Littlefield Publishers, 2005.

Frisbee, John. "A Place Called the Doumer Bridge," *Air Force Magazine*. February 1988: 100.

Goodwin, Kerans. *Lyndon Johnson and the American Dream*. New York: St. Martin's Press, 1991.

Gulf of Tonkin Resolution (1964). Found at https://ourdocuments.gov/doc.php?flash=true&doc=98

Hobson, Chris. *Vietnam Air Losses. United States Air Force, Navy and Marine Corps Fixed-Wing Aircraft Losses in Southeast Asia 1961–1975*. Hinckley, UK: Midland Publishing, 2001.

Johnson, Lyndon. "Report on the Gulf of Tonkin Incident (August 4, 1964)." Found at http://millercenter.org/president/speeches/speech-3998

_____. *The Vantage Point: Perspectives of the Presidency 1963–1969*. New York: Holt, Rinehart and Winston, 1971.

Karnow, Stanley. *Vietnam, A History*. New York: Penguin Random House, 1991.

Lavalle, A. J. C.. "The Tale of Two Bridges and The Battle for the Skies Over North Vietnam." USAF Southeast Asia Monograph Series, Vol. 1. Washington, D.C.: Office of Air Force History, 1985.

LeMay, Curtis. *Mission with LeMay: My Story*. Garden City, NY: Doubleday, 1965.

Levinson, Jeffrey. *Alpha Strike Vietnam: The Navy's Air War 1964 to 1973*. Novato, CA: Presidio Press, 1989.

Logevall, Fredrik. *Embers of War: The Fall of an Empire and the Making of America's Vietnam*. New York: Random House, 2013.

Maitland, T. and Stephen Weiss. *The Vietnam Experience: Raising the Stakes*. Boston: Boston Publishing Company, 1982.

Mersky, Peter. *F-8 Crusader Units of the Vietnam War*. Oxford, UK: Osprey Publishing, 1998.

_____. *U.S. Navy and Marine Corps A-4 Skyhawk Units of the Vietnam War*. Oxford, UK: Osprey Publishing, 2007.

Mersky, Peter and Norman Polmar. *The Naval Air War in Vietnam*. Annapolis, MD: The Nautical and Aviation Publishing Company of America, 1982.

Morgan, Rick. *A-6 Intruder Units of the Vietnam War*. Oxford, UK: Osprey Publishing, 2012.

Morrocco, John. *The Vietnam Experience: Thunder From Above*. Boston: Boston Publishing Company, 1984.

McNamara, Robert. *In Retrospect: The Tragedy and Lessons of Vietnam*. New York: Times Books, 1995.

Naval History Magazine. "Carrier Air and Vietnam," April 1987, Vol. 1, No. 1. *New York Times*. April 21, 1967.

Nichols, John and Barrett Tillman. *On Yankee Station: The Naval Air War over Vietnam*. Annapolis, MD: United States Naval Institute, 1987.

Office of the Secretary of Defense. NPIC Imagery Report J-6976. "Bridge Interdiction North Vietnam." Secret, April 11, 1965.

Olsen, James. *In Country: The Illustrated Encyclopedia of the Vietnam War*. New York: Metro Books, 2008.

Paterson, Pat. "The Truth about Tonkin." *Naval History Magazine*, Vol. 22 (1), February 2008.

Polmar, Norman and Edward Marolda. *Naval Air War: The Rolling Thunder Campaign*. Washington, DC: Naval History and Heritage Command, 2015.

Sharp, U.S. Grant. *Strategy for Defeat: Vietnam in Retrospect*. San Rafael, CA: Presidio Press, 1978.

Smith, John. *Rolling Thunder: The American Strategic Bombing Campaign Against North Vietnam 1964–68*. Walton on Thames, UK: Air Research Publication, 1994.

Taylor, Maxwell. *Swords and Plowshares*. New York: W. W. Norton & Company, 1972.

The Pentagon Papers (Gravel Edition). Vol. I, Ch. 4, "U.S. and France in Indochina, 1950–56." Boston: Beacon Press, 1971.

_____. Vol. III, Ch. 3, "The Air War in North Vietnam: Rolling Thunder Begins, February–June, 1965." Boston: Beacon Press, 1971.

_____. Vol. IV, Ch. 2, "Evolution of the War: Military Pressures Against North Vietnam, November–December 1964." Boston: Beacon Press, 1971.

Toperczer, Istvan. *MiG-17 and MiG-19 Units of the Vietnam War*. Oxford, UK: Osprey Publishing, 2001.

U.S. Department of Defense. Imagery report, CSD/NPIC 214/65. "Railway and Highway Bridge, Thanh Hoa, North Vietnam, 1950N 10548E," Secret, April 29, 1965.

Van Staaveren, Jacob. *Gradual Failure: The Air War over North Vietnam 1965–1966*. Washington, DC: Air Force History and Museum Program, U.S. Air Force, 2002.

Westmoreland, William. *A Soldier Reports*. Garden City, NY: Doubleday & Company, 1976.

(Photo Expert Infantry)

Acknowledgements

Special thanks to the National Museum of the Air Force in Dayton, Ohio and especially to archivist Brett Stolle for his invaluable assistance in helping me research the museum's data and photo collections.

Special thanks to the Naval Aviation Museum in Pensacola, Florida and the volunteer staff of the Emil Buehler Library for their assistance in locating files and photos.

I am grateful to the LBJ Library, the Department of the Air Force, and the Department of the Navy, including the Naval History and Heritage Command in Washington, DC, for their commitment to enhancing public access to official photographic and documentary materials concerning the Vietnam War.

Deep appreciation to all the writers and researchers before me, who have contributed to the large—and growing—body of literature on the air war in Vietnam; much of which I have consulted for this book. Special recognition is given to Chris Hobson's *Vietnam Air Losses*, Douglas Campbell's *U.S. Navy and U.S. Marine Corps Aircraft Damaged or Destroyed During the Vietnam War*, and René Francillon's *Tonkin Gulf Yacht Club*, which are indispensable reference works for anyone delving into the air war in Vietnam.

Finally, to all the men who flew in or supported Operation Rolling Thunder from 1965 to 1968. You had a difficult job to do, but you did it with the highest degree of professionalism to the end.

About the Author

Stephen Emerson was born in San Diego, California into a U.S. Navy family; his father was a career naval aviator and his mother a former Navy nurse. Steve and his siblings grew up on various Navy bases during the Vietnam War. His father served two combat tours in Vietnam flying both the A-4 Skyhawk and the A-7 Corsair II and participated in Operation Rolling Thunder while flying off the USS *Midway* in 1965 with Attack Squadron 22. Steve worked as intelligence analyst covering political-military affairs in Africa and the Middle East before embarking on an academic career. He served as Security Studies Chair at the National Defense University's Africa Center for Strategic Studies and previously as an associate professor of National Security Decision-making at the U.S. Naval War College in Newport, Rhode Island. Steve has written widely on subjects from American national security affairs and political instability to terrorism, African conflicts, and counter-insurgency. Chief among these are his critical assessment of U.S. counter-terrorism policy in Africa, 'The Battle for Africa's Hearts and Minds', and his comprehensive military history of the Mozambican civil war in *The Battle for Mozambique*. He holds a PhD in International Relations/Comparative Politics from the University of Florida and currently resides in Orlando, Florida.